Rigor and Differentiation in the Classroom

Learn how to differentiate instruction while maintaining a rigorous learning environment. In this practical book, rigor expert Barbara R. Blackburn shows that the differentiated classroom doesn't mean extra work for top students and easy work for others; instead, you can have high expectations for all students and provide scaffolding so that everyone can reach success. She also addresses many of the greatest concerns teachers have about implementing differentiated instruction, including:

- ♦ How to manage your time so that you can create lessons, find resources, and grade assignments for students working at different levels;
- ♦ How to balance differentiated instruction and teaching standards;
- ♦ How to ensure rigor at all tiers of instruction;
- ♦ How to collaborate with teachers and other faculty members;
- ♦ How to differentiate homework and other out-of-class assignments;
- ♦ How to explain differentiated instruction to parents and families;
- ♦ And more . . .

Each chapter includes practical tools and activities that you can use immediately to bring all students to higher levels of achievement. Many of these tools are available as eResources and can be downloaded for free from the book's product page: www.routledge.com/9780815394471.

Barbara R. Blackburn, a Top 30 Global Guru in Education, has taught early childhood, elementary, middle, and high school students and has served as an educational consultant for three publishing companies. In addition to speaking at international, national, and state conferences, she also regularly presents workshops for teachers and administrators in elementary, middle, and high schools. She is the author of numerous books, including the bestseller *Rigor Is NOT a Four-Letter Word*.

Rigor and Differentiation in the Classroom

Tools and Strategies

Barbara R. Blackburn

Routledge
Taylor & Francis Group

NEW YORK AND LONDON

First published 2019
by Routledge
711 Third Avenue, New York, NY 10017

and by Routledge
2 Park Square, Milton Park, Abingdon, Oxon, OX14 4RN

Routledge is an imprint of the Taylor & Francis Group, an informa business

Library of Congress Cataloging-in-Publication Data
A catalog record for this title has been requested

ISBN: 978-0-8153-9446-4 (hbk)
ISBN: 978-0-8153-9447-1 (pbk)
ISBN: 978-1-351-18591-2 (ebk)

Typeset in Palatino
by Apex CoVantage, LLC

Visit the eResource: www.routledge.com/9780815394471

Printed and bound in the United States of America by Sheridan

Dedication

This book is dedicated to my editor, Lauren Davis.
Words cannot fully express my admiration for her creativity,
enthusiasm, and dedication to our partnership. I appreciate her
as an editor, but more importantly, as a friend.

Contents

Acknowledgments

My family is always essential to my success. My husband, Pete, is my steadfast love and support. My stepson Hunter inspires me with his strength. My parents have always been positive role models of love and integrity. My sisters, niece, and nephew always encourage me.

Abbigail Armstrong, my former student, a colleague, and my best friend consistently knows exactly what to say. Her husband, son, and daughter also show tremendous patience when I'm having a writing crisis.

Lauren's family also deserves a shout-out for allowing her to prioritize her work with me sometimes when it probably isn't convenient.

Christy Matkovich, my former student and a terrific teacher and assistant principal, shared ideas, especially related to homework. Ron Williamson, Professor of Educational Leadership at Eastern Michigan University, provided information for Chapter 8.

Jessica Bennett and Susan Gorman gave excellent suggestions, which helped me clarify and refine the content.

Emma Capel designed a cover that was just perfect.

Project manager Autumn Spalding and those involved from Apex CoVantage who ensured the final quality of the book.

Finally, I appreciate all the teachers and leaders who work every day to make a difference for students. You amaze me, and I am humbled when you read my work.

eResources

As you read this book, you'll notice the eResources icon ![icon] next to the following tools. The icon indicates that these tools are available as free downloads on our website, www.routledge.com/9780815394471, so you can easily print and distribute them to your students.

Meet the Author

Named a Top 30 Global Guru in Education, Dr. Barbara Blackburn has dedicated her life to raising the level of rigor and motivation for professional educators and students alike. What differentiates Barbara's numerous books are her easily executable, concrete examples based on decades of experience as a teacher, professor, and consultant. Barbara's dedication to education was inspired in her early years by her parents. Her father's doctorate and lifetime career as a professor taught her the importance of professional training. Her mother's career as school secretary shaped Barbara's appreciation of the effort all staff play in the education of every student. Barbara has taught early childhood, elementary, middle, and high school students and has served as an educational consultant for three publishing companies. She holds a master's degree in school administration and was certified as a teacher and school principal in North Carolina. She received her Ph.D. in Curriculum and Teaching from the University of North Carolina at Greensboro. In 2006, she received the award for Outstanding Junior Professor at Winthrop University. She left her position at the University of North Carolina at Charlotte to write and speak full-time.

In addition to speaking at state, national, and international conferences, she also regularly presents workshops for teachers and administrators in elementary, middle, and high schools. Her workshops are lively and engaging and filled with practical information. Her most popular topics include:

- ◆ Rigor Is NOT a Four-Letter Word
- ◆ Rigorous Schools and Classrooms: Leading the Way
- ◆ Rigorous Assessments
- ◆ Differentiating Instruction Without Lessening Rigor in Your Classroom
- ◆ Motivation + Engagement + Rigor = Student Success
- ◆ Rigor for Students With Special Needs
- ◆ Motivating Struggling Students

Barbara can be reached through her website: www.barbarablackburnonline.com

Introduction

As I've worked with teachers and leaders around the world, I've noticed that many educators struggle with differentiation. Common issues include lowering the rigor for struggling students; giving less attention to gifted and advanced students, which means they may not be challenged; and simply trying to manage everything that is needed for implementation.

Two of these have a common thread: not providing rigorous work for students. Since differentiation is designed to meet the needs of all students, no matter where they are on the learning spectrum, it is imperative that we do that without lessening the opportunity for each student to be challenged.

This book addresses that issue. How can we incorporate rigor throughout differentiated instruction? Not just to say that we are doing it—but actually provide each student with rigorous instruction and support each of them so they can be successful?

In Chapter 1, we'll look at the concepts of rigor and differentiation, and I'll describe a combined model for the two. Chapter 2 will provide a description of how to build a learning portrait for each student so that you can differentiate based on students' readiness, interests, cultural aspects, and other characteristics.

In Chapters 3–5, you will find a wealth of strategies for differentiating your expectations, or curriculum; your support and scaffolding, or the process with which students learn; and students' demonstrations of understanding, or products and assessments. Chapter 6 will address how to manage a rigorous, differentiated classroom, including how to build a schedule, utilize space, manage resources, and work with groups.

My favorite is Chapter 7, which is a collection of the most common questions I hear from teachers. For example, the first question is, "*How can I find the time to create lessons, find resources, and grade assignments or tests for students working at all these different levels?*" Throughout Chapters 2–8, you'll see an icon of a clock, which designates that I've provided a time saving tip, but I'll give you a thorough answer in this chapter. If you have concerns about rigor and differentiation, you might skip over to Chapter 7, then return to the other chapters.

We'll finish with strategies for working together in professional learning communities and becoming a teacher-leader in Chapter 8. As you think about the sequence, you'll create a comprehensive plan for implementation.

Plan for Implementation

◆ Build a base of knowledge.

◆ Understand each student's needs through a learning portrait.

◆ Develop instruction that differentiates through expectations, support, and demonstration of learning.

◆ Structure the environment of your classroom.

◆ Read about how to handle potential obstacles.

◆ Work with other teachers for success.

Finally, rigor and differentiation is not a magic formula. It will not guarantee that every single student will reach a particular level of rigor. All will make progress, but perhaps not as much as you would like. Not all students will necessarily score an A or pass the standardized test. However, providing rigorous work with appropriate scaffolding in a differentiated manner will help your students succeed. Keep in mind that implementing rigor and differentiation throughout your classroom instruction takes time. There is a learning curve, and you will absolutely have challenges. You'll try something that doesn't work, or a strategy that works one time won't work another day. That's normal. Keep adjusting to meet students' needs, and you will make a difference.

On your worst day, you are someone's best hope.

Sam Myers,
Sumter School District

1

Rigor and Differentiation

There have been calls for increasing rigor dating back as far as Sputnik in 1957 and continuing with the release of *A Nation at Risk* in 1983. However, in recent years, there has been a renewed emphasis. In 2010, the Common Core State Standards (www.corestandards.org) were created to increase the level of rigor in schools. Other recently revised state standards and newly created national standards similarly reinforced the need. Rigor is at the center of these standards, and much of the push for new standards came from a concern about the lack of rigor in many schools, as well as the need to prepare students for college and careers. There has also been data from sources such as the Programme for International Studies of Assessment (PISA) that have shown us we need to re-evaluate what we are doing in terms of rigor.

Differentiation also has a long history, from as far back as the one-room schoolhouse. However, it gained mainstream popularity with the publication of *The Differentiated Classroom: Responding to the Needs of All Learners* by Dr. Carol Ann Tomlinson in 1999. Based on concerns that the changing needs of a diverse student population were not being met, a model for modifying content, instruction, and assessment for different students led to positive reactions by educators. Although there had been earlier efforts to individualize instruction, differentiated instruction focused on adjusting for small groups of students, rather than creating individual lesson plans for each student. During the last 20 years, teachers have continued to use differentiated instruction to help all students succeed, no matter where they are on the learning spectrum.

However, there have been concerns about differentiated instruction. The most common complaint about differentiation is that, by meeting the needs of students at their level, especially struggling students, teachers lower their expectations and decrease the level of rigor. As one principal shared with me, "I don't think we meant for it to happen, but we are 'dumbing down' instruction for our struggling students and those with special needs."

That is why we need to address the role of rigor in the differentiated classroom. If the goal of differentiation is to help students learn and grow, then we cannot lower the bar just because it is easier for them. Throughout this book, we will look at specific strategies for ensuring that all students, from your most struggling learner to your most advanced one, learn and achieve at high levels that prepare them for life after high school.

In this chapter, we will discuss the myths of rigor, the basic concepts of rigor, beliefs related to rigor, and the role of student motivation in a rigorous classroom. Next, we will turn our attention to differentiation following a similar pattern, addressing myths, concepts, and beliefs. Then we'll finish by looking at a combined model for ensuring rigor in a differentiated classroom.

Rigor

Essentially, rigor is holding each student in your classroom to high expectations and supporting them so they can learn at high levels. In a rigorous classroom, a teacher may begin instruction at a less complicated level, but the goal is always to move students to a deep understanding of complex material.

Myths of Rigor

One of the challenges related to rigor involves the misconceptions about the concept. There are ten commonly held beliefs about rigor that are not true.

Ten Myths About Rigor

Myth 1: Lots of homework is a sign of rigor.

Myth 2: Rigor means doing more.

Myth 3: Rigor is not for younger students.

Myth 4: Rigor is not for struggling students or those with special needs.

Myth 5: When you increase rigor, student motivation decreases.

Myth 6: Providing support means lessening rigor.

Myth 7: Resources equal rigor.

Myth 8: Standards alone take care of rigor.

Myth 9: Rigor means you have to quit doing everything you do now and start over.

Myth 10: Rigor is just one more thing to do.

As you will see in the differentiation section, several of the rigor myths relate to the myths of differentiation.

Concepts of Rigor

In *Rigor Is NOT a Four-Letter Word*, I define rigor as creating an environment in which . . .

♦ each student is expected to learn at high levels,
♦ each student is supported so he or she can learn at high levels, and
♦ each student demonstrates learning at high levels.

Notice we are looking at the environment you create. The tri-fold approach to rigor is not limited to the curriculum students are expected to learn. It is more than a specific lesson or instructional strategy. It is deeper than what a student says or does in response to a lesson. True rigor is the result of weaving together all elements of schooling to raise students to higher levels of learning. Let's take a deeper look at the three aspects of the definition.

Expecting Students to Learn at High Levels

The first component of rigor is creating an environment in which each student is expected to learn at high levels. Having high expectations starts with the recognition that every student possesses the potential to succeed at his or her individual level.

Almost every teacher or leader I talk with says, "We have high expectations for our students." Sometimes that is evidenced by the behaviors in the school; other times, however, faculty actions don't match the words. There are concrete ways to implement and assess rigor in classrooms.

As you design lessons that incorporate more rigorous opportunities for learning, you will want to consider the questions that are embedded in the instruction. Complex, higher level questioning is an integral part of a rigorous classroom.

It is also important to pay attention to how you respond to student questions. When we visit schools, it is not uncommon to see teachers who ask higher level questions. But for whatever reason, we then see some of the same teachers accept low level responses from students. In rigorous classrooms, teachers push students to respond at high levels. They ask extending questions. Extending questions are questions that encourage a student to explain their reasoning and think through ideas. When a student does not know the immediate answer but has sufficient background information to provide a response to the question, the teacher continues to probe and guide the student's thinking rather than moving on to the next student. Insist on thinking and problem-solving.

Supporting Students to Learn at High Levels

High expectations are important, but the most rigorous schools ensure that each student is supported so he or she can learn at high levels, which is the second part of our definition. It is essential that teachers design lessons that move students to more challenging work while simultaneously providing ongoing scaffolding to support students' learning as they move to those higher levels.

Providing additional scaffolding throughout lessons is one of the most important ways to support your students. Oftentimes students have the ability or knowledge to accomplish a task, but are overwhelmed at the complexity of it, therefore getting lost in the process. This can occur in a variety of ways, but it requires that teachers ask themselves during every step of their lessons, "What extra support might my students need?"

Ensuring Students Demonstrate Learning at High Levels

The third component of a rigorous classroom is providing each student with opportunities to demonstrate learning at high levels. There are two aspects to consider. First, each student demonstrates learning. When we lead a discussion, ask a question, and call on a student to respond, only one student demonstrates understanding. In a rigorous lesson, all students show what they have learned, whether through pair-shares, small group discussions, response cards, clickers, exit slips, projects, or other formats.

Additionally, students need to demonstrate that learning at a rigorous level. We'll be looking at this in more depth in later chapters, but for now let's just note that we must expect students to learn at levels of depth and complexity. Not some students, not only the ones who want to learn, not just honors students, but all students.

Beliefs That Support Rigor

Teachers who infuse rigor into their classrooms share similar beliefs.

Rigor and Student Motivation

When I talk with teachers in my workshops, they regularly ask me, "My students don't really care about learning. What is going to happen when I raise the level of rigor?" As a part of increasing rigor in the classroom, we must activate student motivation. Sometimes we try to use extrinsic motivators, such as rewards or grades. They can help, but typically only with rote tasks and they only last a short time. Intrinsic motivation comes from within a student, and builds over time for a long-lasting impact. Students are more motivated when they value what they are doing and when they believe they have a chance for success. Those are the two keys: value and success. Do students see value in the lesson? Do they believe they can be successful?

Value

We typically think of value as the real-life relevance of learning. However, there are three ways students see value in learning. First, relevance is important. Ideally, your students will make their own connections about the relevance of content, and you should provide them opportunities to make those connections independently. But there are also times that you will need to facilitate that understanding. I observed a science teacher who was very effective in helping his students see value in lessons. At the beginning of the year, he asked his students to write about their goals for life after high school. During a lesson on chemical mixtures, he realized that Shaquandra was tuning him out. He asked her, "Why is an understanding of chemical mixtures important to you?" Puzzled, she replied, "I don't know. I don't think it is." He then guided her to a realization that, since she wanted to own a beauty shop, she would need to know about mixtures when using chemical treatments on a customer's hair. Her motivation to participate in the lesson increased tremendously.

However, there are times when we are teaching something that, frankly, really doesn't have any relevance to our students. When I was a teacher, I remember some concepts that I taught only because they were tested at the end of the year. What do we do in that case?

The second way students see value is through activities. Students are more motivated when they are actively engaged in learning. It's important for us to weave purposeful, engaging activities for all students throughout our instruction. Once again, though, there are times when you may not be able to use an activity to teach a particular concept.

Finally, students see value through their relationship with you. No matter their age, students want you to like them. They want to know you care. If you have a positive relationship with your students, they will do their absolute best for you. And if you have a negative relationship with a student, he or she will typically withdraw or act out, and he or she will likely not learn as much.

Success

Success is the second key to student motivation. Students are more motivated when they feel like they are successful or that they have a chance to be successful. If Dustin thinks an assignment is too hard, and that he must complete it on his own, he is likely to give up. But, if he is given a challenge, as well as assurances from you that you will be there to guide and support him, he will try to accomplish the task, and he will likely succeed.

There are a variety of ways to help students be successful, and we will explore those throughout the book. When increasing rigor effectively, teachers thoroughly integrate a focus on success in their classrooms.

Differentiation

Differentiation, which is commonly viewed as a model for meeting students' needs, is more accurately described as a set of beliefs about teaching and learning that are reflected as a set of practices.

Myths of Differentiation

Rick Wormeli, in a Principal Leadership article *Busting Myths About Differentiated Instruction*, shares 10 myths of differentiation.

Ten Myths About Differentiation

Myth 1: Students Will Be Unprepared for Tests

Myth 2: Differentiation Equals Individualization

Myth 3: Differentiation Means Unbalanced Workloads

Myth 4: Lack of Mastery at the Same Time as Classmates Means Lack of Credit

Myth 5: "I Taught It. It's Up to Students to Learn It."

Myth 6: Lesson Plans Must Be Turned In

Myth 7: Summative Assessment Leads to Learning

Myth 8: Students Won't Be Able to Compete in the Real World

Myth 9: If We Don't Differentiate, Students Will Toughen Up

Myth 10: There Is Only One Way to Differentiate

Source: https://www.greatschoolspartnership.org/wp-content/uploads/2017/01/Busting-Myths-About-Differentiated-Instruction-1.pdf

I would add two additional myths: 11) Differentiation Means Students Are Grouped by Ability All the Time and 12) I Can't Implement Differentiation Because It Takes Too Much Time. I always use readiness rather than ability, because I believe in a growth mindset. Students' readiness levels can and will change, and your groupings should reflect that. "Ability" implies that students have an ability level that can never change, no matter what instruction they receive (fixed mindset), which would lead to traditional groupings that label students. Second, it is definitely a challenge to find the time and energy needed for effective differentiation. I'll address this issue in Chapter 7.

Notice how these compare to our myths about rigor. Myth 1, that students will be unprepared for tests, assumes that differentiated instruction is not rigorous. Myth 3, differentiation means unbalanced workloads, parallels the myths related to rigor that more work or extra homework equals rigor. Myth 5, the notion that once a teacher delivers instruction, learning is up to students, contradicts that rigor requires teachers to balance their high expectations with appropriate levels of support.

Concepts of Differentiation

Carol Ann Tomlinson, author of over a dozen books on differentiation and a Professor of Education at the University of Virginia, is a recognized expert on and proponent for differentiation. According to Tomlinson and Marcia Imbeau (2011), differentiation is balancing an emphasis on individual students with course content in the classroom. Differentiated instruction is based on several key tenets.

Key Tenets of Differentiated Instruction

♦ Students differ as learners in terms of background experience, culture, language, gender, interests, readiness to learn, modes of learning, speed of learning, support systems for learning, self-awareness as a learner, confidence as a learner, independence as a learner, and a host of other ways.

♦ Differences profoundly impact how students learn and the nature of scaffolding they will need at various points in the learning process.

♦ Teachers have a responsibility to ensure that all of their students master important content.

♦ Teachers have to make specific and continually evolving plans to connect each learner with key content.

♦ Teachers are required to understand the nature of each of their students, in addition to the nature of the content they teach.

♦ A flexible approach to teaching "makes room" for student variance.

♦ Teachers should continually ask, "What does this student need at this moment in order to be able to progress with this key content, and what do I need to do to make that happen?"

Source: Tomlinson, Carol A., and Imbeau, Marcia B. (2011). *Leading and Managing a Differentiated Classroom*. Alexandria, VA: Association for Supervision and Curriculum Development.

In a differentiated classroom, the teacher modifies three areas in order to improve learning for all students: content, process, and product.

Modifications in the Differentiated Classroom

Area to Be Modified	Description
Content	What students learn (knowledge, skills, and understandings)
Process	Instruction (how students learn)
Product	How students demonstrate understanding (assessments)

Recently, Dr. Tomlinson has added a fourth area, affect, which relates to how students' feelings and emotions affect their learning. We will address affective elements within the concept of student motivation. Next, decisions about what and how to differentiate instruction are based on three student factors: readiness, interest, and learning profile.

Basis for Modification

Vary by	Description
Readiness	Does not represent ability, rather is a changing state of skill level
Interest	Areas of interest for a student
Learning Profile	Preferred ways of learning, which include learning styles, multiple intelligences, gender, and culture

Beliefs That Support Differentiation

Teachers who incorporate differentiation hold shared beliefs.

- Students are individuals with different skills, interests, styles, talents, strengths, and weaknesses.
- Every student deserves an equitable opportunity for high quality learning in a respectful manner.
- Differences in students are significant enough to make a major impact on what students need to learn, the pace at which they need to learn it, and the support they need from teachers and others to learn it well.
- Instruction should be tailored to students' readiness levels, interests, and learning profiles.
- Most students can master most essential concepts when the teacher maximizes the capacity of each learner.

Rigor and Differentiation: A Winning Combination

Combined Beliefs

For teachers who want to incorporate both rigor and differentiation in their classrooms, there are five key beliefs. When we focus on the steps to implement rigorous, differentiated instruction without addressing the necessary philosophy that drives that instruction, we dilute our efforts.

Shared Beliefs About Rigor and Differentiation

- Every student deserves an equitable opportunity to learn at rigorous levels, which includes providing appropriate support.
- Students can learn essential, rigorous, complex concepts when teachers meet students where they are and help them move forward.
- Students are individuals who have different needs, strengths, and weaknesses.
- We should create a classroom environment and instruction that addresses all aspects of students' needs.

How Rigor and Differentiation Work Together

In order to ensure that a differentiated classroom is truly rigorous, we can blend the two concepts together into a new framework. First, let's take our definition of rigor and overlay its aspects on the three ways to differentiate.

Aspects of Rigor	*Ways to Differentiate*
Expectations	Content
Support	Process
Demonstration of Learning	Product

We will look at what has traditionally been called differentiation by "content" as options for adjusting facets related to expectations, while still keeping the expectations high. "Process," or instruction, from a rigor standpoint is how to adjust the amount and type of support needed for students to be successful. And "product," or assessment, is how students demonstrate they understand key concepts.

Next, the traditional differentiation model recommends varying the content, process, and product based on readiness, interest, and learning profile. What I've found is that if we address all aspects of student motivation, we will have a comprehensive plan for adjusting our expectations, support, and demonstration of learning.

Motivational Elements	*Differentiation Model*
Chance of Success	Readiness
Value	Interest
Success and Value	Learning Profile

A Final Note

Throughout this book, we will address differentiation through the eyes of rigor, as described on the previous page. In Chapter 2, we will explore the concept of a learning portrait. In Chapters 3, 4, and 5, we will discuss differentiating by expectations, support, and demonstration of learning. Managing the rigorous, differentiated classroom is the topic of Chapter 6. Chapter 7 will investigate a range of challenges related to differentiation, such as how to implement rigorous differentiation with limited time and resources, grading, and communicating with parents and families. Chapter 8 concludes with a discussion of teacher leadership for change. In Chapters 2–6, whenever you see a clock icon, I've provided a time management tip to help smooth the process. Let's start our journey.

 ### *Points to Ponder*

The most important thing I learned was . . .

I was surprised about . . .

I want to learn more about . . .

I'd like to try . . .

2

Learning Portraits

As I was writing this book, I saw two pictures that helped me think about this chapter. The first was a profile of a young child. Although it was a nice picture, I didn't have a full view of the boy. Beside it was a picture of the same boy, this time in a portrait. I could see all of his face, and it gave me a better representation of who he was.

I realized that portraits are far more helpful than profiles in terms of understanding who someone is.

In order to differentiate rigorous instruction, you need to have a portrait of each student. How can you know what and how to adjust instruction if you don't have a complete picture of each of your students? In order to create a portrait to help you fully understand all aspects of each student, you'll want to use a mix of formal and informal strategies to gather detailed information related to a variety of areas.

Areas for Learning Portrait

- ◆ Readiness
- ◆ Ability
- ◆ Interest
- ◆ Culture
- ◆ Maslow's Hierarchy of Needs
- ◆ Social and Emotional Learning
- ◆ Growth Mindset

Time Management Tip

 Collect your information a bit at a time. Start with what already exists, such as standardized testing information, and add to it over time.

Readiness

The readiness level of each student is probably the most important aspect of a learning portrait. The heart of teaching is to take a student from where he or she is and move him or her to a higher level of learning. To do that, you need to understand where a student is in terms of knowledge and understanding. There are less formal ways to do this, such as anticipation guides, and there are more formal strategies, such as pre-tests. Ideally, you assess readiness levels before you start units or lessons, and you continue to assess changing readiness levels using formative assessments.

Anticipation Guides

Anticipation guides allow you to see a snapshot of what students know and don't know about the content for a specific lesson or topic. They are simple to use, and student-friendly.

Anticipation Guide

Name _____ Date _____

Title of story _____ Author _____

Anticipation Guide				

Use the following anticipation guide to preview a story before you read it. Before reading, mark whether or not you agree or disagree with each statement. After reading the story, fill in the page number where you found the answer to each statement, tell whether or not you were right, and reflect on what you found.

	Agree/Disagree	Page #	Were you right?	Reflect
1.				
2.				
3.				
4.				
5.				
6.				
7.				

Credit line: This resource was provided by ReadWriteThink.org, a website developed by the National Council of Teachers of English. ReadWriteThink aims to provide educators and students access to the highest quality practices and resources in reading and language arts instruction.

Anticipation Guide Version 2

Credit line: This resource was provided by ReadWriteThink.org, a website developed by the National Council of Teachers of English. ReadWriteThink aims to provide educators and students access to the highest quality practices and resources in reading and language arts instruction.

Time Management Tip

Anticipation Guides are helpful, and you can streamline your time if you create a template and simply add in the statements each time.

Pre-Tests

I've known teachers who use a pre-test for the year, using a broad range of questions to identify topics that might need less instruction. A far more effective approach, in my experience, is to use pre-testing to measure students' understanding of each key topic (which usually means a learning unit, such as a two-week study of landforms).

Characteristics of an Effective Pre-Test

♦ Focuses on essential skills

♦ Incorporates questions that determine if students understand necessary background knowledge

♦ Incorporates questions that determine if students understand concepts planned for instruction

♦ Incorporates questions that determine if students have advanced knowledge of concepts

♦ Is not overwhelming for students

♦ Uses questions that are clear and understandable

Time Management Tip

 If you are using a textbook, it may have accompanying pre-tests as a part of resource support. You may also have access to a computer program that can help you measure readiness.

Ongoing Formative Assessments to Gauge Readiness

Assessing students' readiness at the beginning of a lesson or unit isn't enough to differentiate on an ongoing basis. It simply provides you a base of information. Students' readiness levels change over time, and you need to assess those changes. That is the role of formative assessment. There are a variety of options you can use.

Sample Formative Assessments

♦ Observations

♦ Interviews and Conferences

♦ Ways to Summarize Information

♦ Using Movement

♦ Metacognitive Assessments

Observations

An important formative assessment tool for teachers is the use of observations. Observations can be planned, or they can be spontaneous. In an observation, you simply observe what students are doing and take notes for documentation. You may choose to observe for particular instructional behaviors or you may simply observe to see what happens from a general standpoint. Checklists, which provide a quick way for you to make notes about your observations, can be simple yes/no tallies or they can be open-ended for teachers to add notes.

Sample Math Checklist	
Characteristic	*Notes*
Student demonstrates problem-solving ability.	
Student demonstrates persistence while solving problems.	
Student reflects on his/her thinking.	
Student shows applications of learning to real life.	

Time Management Tip

Definitely use a checklist when observing students. If it helps, use a grid, so you can put your criteria on the rows and students' names in the columns. This will save time and focus your observation.

Interviews and Conferences

In interviews and conferences, the teacher meets with students to assess understanding of content. For either of these, the teacher plans a series of questions to ask a student about his or her learning. It's also important to stay flexible and adjust questions during the interview or conference. They are probably used most often in writing situations, but they can be used with any subject area.

Time Management Tip

Although interviews are an excellent way to collect individual information, you can also do small group conferences with four or five students. This helps you manage your time while still gaining valuable information.

Ways to Summarize Information

3× Summaries

Ask students to write three summaries, one at a time. The first one is a summary written in 10–15 words, the next one is 30–50 words, and the final one is 75–100 words. You may start with the smallest number of words, which allows students to build on that information, or start with the largest, which requires students to winnow down to the most important information. With younger students, you might use a picture, a word, and a sentence.

Postcards

As a historical figure or a character in a book or story, write a postcard to another historical figure or character describing an event and why it is important to the story or situation.

Appointment Clock

The Appointment Clock can be embedded within a lesson. The teacher places students in groups of three. At teacher-designated points in the lesson (such as every 15 minutes), they go to their appointment to share their learning with the other members of the group or answer a question asked by the teacher. The teacher walks around and listens to the conversations taking place between partners, noting any misconceptions or misunderstandings. The teacher uses this information to adjust instruction by redirecting the next segment of the lesson to assist students in their learning.

Roll the Die

Put a die at each desk. At the end of class, each student rolls the die and briefly answers aloud a question based on the number rolled. This becomes the exit slip for the day.

Prompts Based on Numbers on Dice

1. I want to remember . . .
2. Something I learned today
3. One word to sum up what I learned
4. Something I already knew
5. I'm still confused about . . .
6. An "aha" moment that I had today

Electronic Exit Slips

You may already use exit slips or exit tickets, which are simple response forms for students to complete at the end of class. These can range from simple, as in "What did you learn," to more complex with multiple questions. With today's technology, there are a variety of ways to collect this information from your students.

Electronic Exit Slips

- Google Forms
- Plickers
- Twitter
- Socrative
- Geddit
- Poll Everywhere
- ExitTicket
- Voice Thread
- Lino
- Padlet

Time Management Tip

 Any of the ideas for summarizing content can be done quickly. They shouldn't take 20 minutes. Build them in as a regular routine so students become accustomed to them.

Using Movement

Another way to assess students' understanding of content is to use movement. If you are reviewing multiple-choice questions, you can use Four Corners, in which students move to a corner of the room based on their answers. Then, discuss the responses and give students an opportunity to switch corners. You can also do Forced Choice, where students have to make a choice as to whether they agree or disagree with a position or statement. Have students move to one side of the room or the other. Then, have each group discuss their choice and their justification for the choice. You can tailor movement to your specific needs.

Math Graphing Example

To determine whether or not students have an understanding of how to plot points on a coordinate plane, the teacher can use this formative assessment. A coordinate plane is created on the classroom floor or other large area and the x-axis and y-axis are labeled. The plane can contain four quadrants or just one, depending on the level of the students. Students are seated around the outside of the grid on the floor. A student draws a card containing a pair of coordinates and must decide where on the grid to stand. Once the student has determined where to stand, he/she must explain how he/she arrived at that position. If the student has moved to an incorrect position, he/she may call on a partner to help figure out where to relocate.

Time Management Tip
While these are great formative assessments, they also allow students to take a break from sitting and burn up excess energy. Plan accordingly.

Metacognitive Assessments

You may want to know how students feel about their own understanding. A teacher in one of my workshops shared "Which Road Are You On?"

- The Dirt Road (There's so much dust, I can't see where I'm going! Help!!)
- The Paved Road (It's fairly smooth, but there are many potholes along the way.)
- The Highway (I feel fairly confident but have an occasional need to slow down.)
- The Interstate (I'm traveling along and could easily give directions to someone else.)

Another strategy is a "Hand Thermometer." Students raise their hands to show you how well they understand the content. All the way up is "hot" or excellent; half way up is "mild" or okay, but could be better; just above desk height is "cold" or needs to be improved.

Time Management Tip
Use these as very quick whole group scans. With the roads, simply ask all students if they are on the dirt road (hands up), paved road (hands up), etc. With the hand thermometer, all students respond at the same time.

Ability or Mastery

Many people believe that the ability level of a student is the most important indicator of a student's performance. My challenge with that belief is that it reflects a fixed mindset rather than a growth mindset.

This is why I will consider standardized testing and IQ tests, but they are not the most important information in a students' learning portrait.

Areas to Be Modified

Fixed Mindset vs. Growth Mindset	
Fixed Mindset	*Growth Mindset*
A student has a set ability that cannot be changed. He or she performs based on that ability.	No matter where they are currently performing academically, students can learn and grow.

Standardized Tests

Standardized tests provide a one-time snapshot of student performance. They do not show you a full picture of what a student knows; rather, they give you an idea of how students perform in a high-stakes environment, demonstrating their understanding of content in a structured format. Because of the design of the tests by psychometricians, they are considered valid and reliable. However, as you probably know from your own experience, life is not always valid and reliable. Students may buckle under the stress of high-stakes testing, they may be dealing with a crisis at home, or they simply may not care how they score, so they randomly answer questions. I've personally seen each of these occur. While not perfect, they do provide a gauge of what a student knows at a certain point in time. Many people consider them to be a measure of ability; I prefer to think of them as one picture of mastery of a comprehensive set of understanding.

Let's take a brief look at information about standardized testing. I'm not going to go in-depth, because you probably are already overwhelmed with information about testing, especially in our high-stakes testing environment. However, in a guide for parents, the Lane Education Service District in Oregon provides a succinct overview of key points (www.lesd. k12.or.us/homeschooling/documents/testing-assessment/Parent%27s% 20Guide%20to%20 Understanding%20Achievement%20Testing.pdf).

Purposes of Standardized Testing

Standardized tests are not the final and complete evaluation of a student's learning, although you may certainly feel that way in today's environment. However, most teachers understand there is more to a student than a single test score.

Achievement Tests Can:	*Achievement Tests Can't:*
◆ Measure your child's ability to recall certain facts, basic skills, and concepts common to the grade tested. ◆ Compare your child's scores with other students' scores. ◆ Assess your child's year-to-year development of learning, if the same test is used for several years.	◆ Tell you if your child has achieved academically to the level of his/her ability. ◆ Measure your child's many other skills and abilities not on the test.

♦ Help you determine your child's academic strengths and weaknesses, as well as the effectiveness of the curriculum, teaching methods, or emphasis, when results are combined with your own observations.	♦ Replace your own informed evaluation of your child's knowledge and skills gained from your daily observation of his work and more thorough and frequent review questions.

Types of Standardized Testing

For many years, the use of norm-referenced tests was the way schools determined student success. Tests such as the California Achievement Test (CAT) and the Iowa Test of Basic Skills (ITBS) were commonly used, and often the scores were used to place students in leveled classes, creating a tracking system. Today, we find a mix of norm-referenced and criterion-referenced testing, with a stronger focus on criterion-referenced tests. Most teachers find criterion-referenced testing to be more useful in understanding what students know and what they still need to learn, as long as they receive detailed information about the results.

Criterion-Referenced Test	*Norm-Referenced Test*
Criterion-referenced tests are designed to measure student performance against a fixed set of predetermined standards to assess whether students have learned a specific set of objectives. If students perform at or above the established expectations, they will pass the test, meet the expected standards, or be deemed "proficient." On a criterion-referenced test, every student taking the exam could theoretically fail if they don't meet the expected standard; alternatively, every student could earn the highest possible score.	Norm-referenced tests measure basic concepts and skills commonly taught in schools throughout the country. These tests are not designed to measure a specific curriculum, but rather the knowledge generally taught at a particular grade level. Results from a norm-referenced test compare a student's performance to a national reference group (the "norm") of students at the same grade. Individual results on these tests are usually reported as a percentage or percentile. A percentile rank indicates the percentage of the norm obtaining scores equal to or less than the test-taker's score. A percentile score does not refer to the percentage of questions answered correctly. Instead, it indicates the test-taker's standing relative to the norm group standard.

Note: Information for these two definitions also collated from public knowledge about the two types of tests.

Some standardized tests do provide diagnostic information, or information that allows you to understand students' strengths and weaknesses. Those are more useful for you to improve your instruction. Be sure to find out if the standardized test your state, district, or school uses can be used as a diagnostic tool.

Understanding Types of Scores

Finally, consider definitions of basic terminology used in tests. You may have multiple scores from a test; be sure you know what each means.

Types of Scores and What They Mean

♦ *Raw Scores:* A raw score is the number of items answered correctly on a given test. Raw scores by themselves have little or no meaning. A child's raw score (number correct) is compared to the original group of students of the same age who first took the test. The averages of this original group are called the "Norms." Norm-referenced test scores compare a child's raw score to those of the norm group. Next, a child's raw scores are converted into scaled scores, grade equivalents, percentiles, and stanines.

♦ *Scaled Score:* A scaled score is a mathematical transformation of a raw score. Scaled scores are useful when comparing test results over time. Most standardized achievement test batteries provide scaled scores for such purposes. Several different methods of scaling exist, but each is intended to provide a continuous score scale across the different forms and levels of a test series.

♦ *Grade Equivalent:* This is the most commonly misunderstood term in interpreting test scores. The first digit represents the year of the grade level and the digit after the decimal represents the month of the grade level. If a second grader gets a 5.4, it does not mean the child is ready for fifth grade. It just means that an average fifth grader would have scored as well on the same test. It also lets you know the second grader mastered the material very well and answered most questions correctly.

♦ *Percentile:* This score ranks individuals within a group on a scale of 1–99 with 50 being average. A student cannot score 100% because he or she cannot score better than himself or herself. A percentile rank of 75 means the student scored better than 75 % of the other students in his or her norm group, and 25 %

---

scored as well or better than your student. It does not mean the student got 75% of the items correct. Percentile does not refer to the percent of questions that were answered correctly.

- ◆ *Stanine:* This term comes from the combination of the words "standard of nine." It rates a child's achievement on a scale of 1–9 based on a coarse grouping of the scores. In general, a stanine of 1, 2, or 3 indicates below average achievement. A stanine of 4, 5, or 6 indicates average achievement, while a 7, 8, or 9 indicates above average.

Time Management Tip

You may have a clear understanding of the standardized test that is typically provided by the state. If you don't, check out the state department website, and look for the Frequently Asked Questions. Also, see if they provide information for parents; I find it to be more concise and written in more practical terms.

Interest

Another aspect of differentiating instruction is to incorporate students' interests. You may give students opportunities to connect their learning to their interests or group students by interest for a project.

Sample Assignment That Incorporates Interest

Throughout this semester, we've learned about a variety of math concepts. Choose something you are interested in, and create a project that shows how math is important to your interest. For example, if you like skateboarding, you might create a video that shows the geometry aspects of skateboarding.

In addition to simply asking students about their interests, you may want to have them answer an interest inventory at the beginning of the year to help you understand what they like.

Sample Questions for Interest Inventory

- What is your favorite thing to do after school?
- What do you like to read about?
- What movies or TV shows do you like?
- What kind of music do you like?
- Do you like to work by yourself or with someone?
- What pets do you have or what animals do you like?
- What is your favorite subject?
- What is your least favorite subject?
- What do you want to do after high school?
- What is something you are proud of?
- If I had one wish, it would be . . .
- What is your favorite hobby?
- I'm really good at . . .
- I really liked it when one of my teachers . . .
- I didn't like it when one of my teachers . . .
- Is there anything else you want to tell me?

Sample Format for Interest Inventory for Primary Students

Statements	Yes	No
I like school.	☺	☹
I like to read.	☺	☹
I like to write stories.	☺	☹
I like math.	☺	☹
I like making things.	☺	☹

Learning about science is fun.	☺	☹
I like animals.	☺	☹
I like to work with my friends.	☺	☹

Time Management Tip

A simple way to find about students' interests is to simply ask them, or use an exit slip for them to tell you about their interests. It's also a time saver to use Google Docs or another technology tool.

Culture

Culture is an important part of building a portrait of your students. One of the biggest misconceptions about addressing students' cultural needs is thinking that mentioning a student's culture—for instance, talking or reading about a famous Hispanic figure—is enough. Being responsive to students' cultures encompasses many areas, from your own beliefs, to understanding and responding to your students. For example, a common cultural tradition that cuts across many groups, such as African American, Latino, Southeast Asian, and Pacific Islander communities, is the use of oral language. Oftentimes, story telling is a critical part of how they learn. They use memory strategies to make learning stick, connecting what needs to be remembered to a rhythm or music (which is why the ABC song is so popular). If we understand this, we can use that information to help all students learn.

Check Out Your Personal Beliefs

The first step to working with students from culturally and linguistically diverse backgrounds is to discover your own biases. Linda Ross (n.d.) gives us some guiding questions.

Examples of Aspects of Cultures

African-American	Hispanic	Asian-American	Pacific Islander
African cultures are represented in many forms of music, dance, art, and storytelling. With more than 1,000 languages spoken and many different religions and tribes, Africa is rich in cultural diversity. African American homes also have remarkable diversity, with notable differences across regions of the U.S. Families often include immediate and extended relatives, with a group-oriented worldview and a strong sense of shared community. For this and other cultures that value a lifestyle of cooperation and sharing,	The term *Hispanic* is used in the United States to describe all people of Latino and Spanish descent. It is a broad ethnic classification of people originating from over 20 countries in Central and South America. Educators need to account for diversity among Hispanic students. The family is the nucleus of Hispanic life. Involving the family as much as possible in the education process will not only help the student, but also increase the likelihood of future educational success among all family members.	Asian Americans commonly face challenges in establishing cultural identity, especially second-generation immigrants who struggle to balance traditional cultural ideas with the pressure of assimilating into American cultural society. When working with individuals of Asian ancestry, educators need to understand three of the main Eastern philosophies and their impact on Asian culture: Buddhism, Confucianism, and Taoism. Within these philosophies, families are highly structured,	The Pacific Islanders live a very social lifestyle, in which family members, both immediate and extended, work together in a solidified community. Pacific Islanders often have difficulty balancing their traditional "laid-back" lifestyles with the high pressure competitive demands of American pedagogy and marketplace economy. Pacific Islanders' cultures follow customs and traditions based on ancient principles that promote living an honorable and noble lifestyle. Embedded deeply into the Polynesian

activities that involve tactile learning and cooperative grouping may be particularly effective, as they parallel the context for learning found in the cultures.

Many Hispanic students are bilingual. If they are not proficient in their native language or the language spoken at home, they may have difficulty with English language skills or reading comprehension in school. Hispanics tend to have closer personal space and value physical contact. Appearance and group memberships are very important. Latinos will work hard for the goals of a group and will work hard for the needs of the community.

hierarchical, and paternal. Within the family systems children are taught that they must avoid bringing shame to their family and that the welfare and integrity of the family are very important. These Asian philosophies also teach principles of peace, balance, and harmony, causing some Asians to avoid confrontation or appear passive, indifferent, or indecisive. Using indirect methods of communication may be appropriate for some Asian students with strong ties to their ancestral culture.

culture are traditional music, dance, and food. Cultural storytelling, music, and dance are ancient ways of passing down history from one generation to another. Thus, teachers with students who are Pacific Islanders may want to use both written and oral instruction, particularly in areas of literacy.

Source: http://education.byu.edu/diversity/culture

Source: http://www.scholastic.com/teachers/article/connect-kids-and-parents-different-cultures-0

Understanding Different Cultures

It's important to understand the different cultures of your students. There are many sources that provide information about varying groups. Although these may be a starting point, keep in mind that students are individuals, and broad generalizations about culture may not apply to them.

Ways Culture Can Affect Behavior

How Culture Affects Behavior

1. **Speaking Up:** Sociologists draw a distinction between "high context" societies in which there are many rules and people say less and "low context" societies that depend on explicit verbal messages. For example, some students will not speak up during a class discussion because when adults lead a discussion, they are used to listening and only speaking when asked a question.

2. **Tracking Time:** There are also different cultural takes on time: monochronic, meaning that people do one thing at a time and adhere to schedules, and polychronic, in which people do several things at a time, put interpersonal needs over schedules, and may view time as an invasion of self. Also, some cultures view

showing up at the start of an event as an imposition; in other cultures, it would be rude to be late.

3. **Physical Self:** Culture shapes the kinds of gestures we use—for example, beckoning someone is offensive in some cultures—and the amount of personal space we need to feel comfortable. This has an impact on how you arrange for groupings and design work spaces.

4. **Personal Interaction:** Importantly for teachers, our cultures also contribute to how we view cooperation, competition, and discipline. Once again, this impacts how and how often you group students.

Learn About Your Students' Individual Cultures

A creative way to learn about all your students is through the use of Culture Boxes. At the beginning of the year, ask your students to put 7–10 items that represent different aspects of who they are into a shoebox. Your students will love this activity, so visit your local shoe store and get lots of shoeboxes of varying sizes. You'll have at least one student who needs the large, boot-sized box. As Charlesetta Dawson explains:

These objects reflect their family heritage, origins, ethnicity, language, religion, hobbies, and likes (foods, music, literature, movies, sports, etc.). The outsides of the boxes are decorated with pictures, symbols, and words/phrases to further explain who they are. Then the students share their culture boxes with the class. Every semester, my students always say that creating a culture box was their favorite activity because they got to be creative, share previously unknown information about themselves with their peers and teacher, and develop a better understanding of the similarities that we all have in common. The sharing might take more than one class period, but the time spent is well worth it!

Another option I have used is the creation of "Me Posters." Students create their posters at the start of the year. I adapted this idea from one my dad used with teachers during workshops. I provided some starting points, using basic pictures or shapes, and students could customize the posters. This gave me a tremendous amount of information about who they were and their interests and goals—probably more than I would have known if I had merely talked with them or asked them to write about themselves because many were reluctant writers.

Components of Me Poster

- Star—In what way are you a star?

- Trading Stamp—What part of your personality would you like to trade in?

- Flower Pot—How can you make our classroom a better place to be?

- First Prize Ribbon—For what one thing would you like to be remembered?

- Crown—What is your crowning achievement?

- Winner—Why are you a winner?

- Turkey—What are the turkeys that get you down?

- Question Mark—What one thing do you want others to know about you?

- Arrow—What is one thing you want to accomplish this year?

- Hands—What do you want me to know about your family?

Time Management Tip

 Don't use these activities just with your culturally diverse students. That isolates them and can be a negative experience. If you do the activities with everyone, you don't have to plan two separate lessons, and you find out more about everyone in your class.

Build Relationships

Understanding students' cultures helps you build relationships with your students. It demonstrates that you care about students. However, that is not enough. You'll want to continue to connect with your students by asking them questions about their lives, involving their families, and finding other ways to connect, such as attending events in which they are participating. Probably the most important action you can take with students from diverse cultures is to learn how to pronounce their names correctly. That sounds basic, but it shows respect for your students.

Reflect Different Cultures in Your Classroom

Take a moment to look at your walls and the teaching materials you use. Do they represent the diversity of your students? If you have Latino or Hispanic students, are there posters on your wall of role models who look like them? If you teach African-American students, are they represented in your textbooks and other reading materials? We can't just spend one day on a culture and say we are responding to our students. We must integrate their cultures into our instruction. When you bring in guest speakers, be sure they reflect the diversity of your classroom. This may include inviting speakers who are first-generation college graduates, reading books about the first African-American woman in space, or using videos for students to experience various cultures.

You'll also want to consider whether your instructions are culturally sensitive. One of my student teachers was working with a small group of students, two of whom were Hispanic and had recently moved to the United States. They were reviewing fractions, and students seemed to be making progress. Then, they were given a worksheet with several word problems to complete. Immediately, students showed confusion and stopped working. The issue was not their lack of understanding fractions; it was the wording of the first question:

If you have 1/2 box of Twinkies, how many Twinkies do you have?

The students had no idea what Twinkies, a cream-filled snack cake, were, or that they are boxed in sets of 10. They would have been able to do the math if they had understood the question. Think about what you do with your students and make sure you are not doing anything that becomes a stumbling block to learning. Consider whether or not your students need context and, if so, provide it for them.

Time Management Tip

Don't tackle integrating cultural responsiveness into your instruction in a huge, time-consuming chunk at the beginning of the year. Instead, make your adjustments as a regular part of your planning, so you spread out the work.

Teach Students About Differences Between Their Culture and School Culture

Several years ago, a teacher shared with me a story about her students. She explained that many of her students came from culturally diverse backgrounds, and some did not understand the difference between using formal language and slang language in the classroom.

One day, she brought two items with her to class: a swimsuit and a black dress. She asked her students where she should wear the swimsuit. She then explained she would be attending a funeral the next day; should she wear the swimsuit there? The students immediately responded, "No. You should wear the dress." She used that example to explain the difference between using formal language and more expressive slang. There's a place for each, but you have to pick and choose your times.

I thought that was an excellent example of dealing with cultural diversity. Too often, we simply reprimand students for something that is from their culture rather than trying to bridge the gap.

Connecting With Families

In many cultures, family is an important part of students' lives. However, you may need to connect differently with families from different cultures. For example, in some cultures, relationships are more important than information. Therefore, when you meet with parents and families (and with your students), you must build a relationship before you share information. Try to find commonalities and show interest in the student both inside and outside the classroom. Another item for consideration is that in some cultures, extended family is important, so you may want to connect with more than just parents.

Another strategy that is effective is to ask families to help you understand their children, young adolescents, and adolescents. You are simply asking them what they would like you to know about their family member. They can write you a letter, cut out pictures from magazines (you may need to provide), write a few words (you may want to provide a list of words they can circle), take pictures, tell you verbally, or record a video. Your goal is to meet families where they are, and that means providing multiple options to give you the information. You may also need to find different ways to connect with them to get the information, whether that is by sending something home on paper, using technology, calling families, or even visiting them at home or in a neutral location if they are uncomfortable with a home visit. I've known teachers who coordinate with a local church and others who meet families at McDonald's. We'll discuss strategies for involving families in Chapter 7, but before you jump into "school business" with families, seek to connect with them on a personal level.

Maslow's Hierarchy of Needs

Abraham Maslow (1943) identified a hierarchy of needs that people experience.

Maslow's Hierarchy	
◆ Self-Actualization	◆ Safety
◆ Esteem	◆ Physiological
◆ Love/Belonging	

Maslow proposed that before one can focus on the need for knowledge or understanding (self-actualization), the lower level needs, such as esteem, belonging, security, and survival must be met. For example, if I'm a student attending a new school, I care more about finding my classroom than I do about today's lesson. As you see, his work applies to student learning. Let's adapt his material a bit to consider how this might look in a classroom. Our goal is self-actualization, in which students focus on learning first. But notice all the other learning needs that must be met.

Needs Identified by Maslow	*Application to Students*
Aesthetic (Self-Actualization)	Am I focused on my own learning and confident in myself?
Need for Understanding Need for Knowledge	Do I understand the content enough so I can explain it to others? Do I understand what I don't know so I can try to discover that information? What facts or concepts do I need to know? What would I like to know about this topic? What level of support will I have? Do I know where to go for help?

(Continued)

(Continued)

Needs Identified by Maslow	Application to Students
Esteem Needs Belonging Needs	Will I be successful? Do I have the knowledge and skills for success? Will other students think I'm good in school? Do other students like me? Does my teacher like me? Does he or she think I belong in his or her classroom? What will others think of me if I work hard? Do I have any friends?
Security Needs Survival Needs	Do I have a place to sit? Do I like who is around me? What happens if I don't know the answer? Will other students make fun of me? What will my teacher say? Will he or she help me? Do I have time to get to my next class? Do I know my locker combination? Did I have breakfast this morning? Will I be able to eat lunch? Do I have the supplies I need to do my work? If we are going to go outside, do I have a jacket? Do I have what I need at home to do my homework? Can I get to the library if I need to?

Relationship of the Hierarchy of Needs to Poverty

Students who live in poverty are often limited to the survival level of Maslow's hierarchy because of their situation.

Types of Poverty

Type	Impact for Teachers
Situational poverty	Generally caused by a sudden crisis or loss and is often temporary. Events causing situational poverty include environmental disasters, divorce, or severe health problems.

Type	Impact for Teachers
Generational poverty	Occurs in families where at least two generations have been born into poverty. Families living in this type of poverty are not equipped with the tools to move out of their situations.
Absolute poverty	Is rare in the United States and involves a scarcity of such necessities as shelter, running water, and food. Families who live in absolute poverty tend to focus on day-to-day survival.
Relative poverty	Refers to the economic status of a family whose income is insufficient to meet its society's average standard of living.
Urban poverty	Occurs in metropolitan areas with populations of at least 50,000 people. The urban poor deal with a complex aggregate of chronic and acute stressors (including crowding, violence, and noise) and are dependent on often-inadequate large-city services.
Rural poverty	Occurs in nonmetropolitan areas with populations below 50,000. In rural areas, there are more single-guardian households, and families often have less access to services, support for disabilities, and quality education opportunities. Programs to encourage transition from welfare to work are problematic in remote rural areas, where job opportunities are few. The rural poverty rate is growing and has exceeded the urban rate every year since data collection began in the 1960s.

Source: Eric Jensen, *Engaging Students With Poverty in Mind* (2013)

There is a limit to how much you can address the issues surrounding poverty, as many aspects of poverty are societal. However, we cannot address those concerns here. Although the differentiated support and scaffolding ideas we will discuss in Chapter 4 can help you address needs of students in poverty, there are some general strategies that will particularly benefit students living in poverty.

Strategies for Teaching Students in Poverty

♦ Build a personal relationship.

♦ Listen so you truly understand the student.

♦ Assess each student's resources.

♦ Give students a sense of control.

♦ Use a calm voice.

♦ Teach social and emotional learning skills.

♦ Teach hope and growth mindset.

♦ Build vocabulary and background knowledge.

♦ Boost engagement.

Time Management Tip

 Ask for help in addressing students' survival needs. One teacher I worked with in an elementary school provided a different way for students to complete a project. She bought several lunch boxes (finding used ones at yard sales and garage sales and then sanitizing them). She filled the boxes with the assignment and all the materials they needed to complete the assignment. She provided this for any student who did not have materials at home in a positive manner. She also worked with a local non-profit group to provide a backpack of standard resource materials at the beginning of the year and at mid-year so they had what they needed.

Social and Emotional Learning

We are continuing to learn about the importance of social and emotional learning related to academic learning. There are five areas of social-emotional learning.

Characteristics of Social-Emotional Learning

♦ Self-Awareness

♦ Self-Management

♦ Social Awareness

♦ Relationship Skills

♦ Responsible Decision-Making

Understanding students' social-emotional strengths and weaknesses helps you make differentiated decisions related to whether students will be more successful working individually or in groups. You can simply observe students to identify aspects of students' social-emotional learning, or you can use a self-assessment. With younger students, you may need to simplify the language or read the items to students.

Social-Emotional Learning Self-Assessment			
Self-Awareness			
	I don't think so	*I'm working on it*	*I'm good at it*
I know what I'm good at and what I need to work on.			
When I'm upset, I can tell why.			
I believe I can do well as long as I focus and try hard.			

(Continued)

(Continued)

Social-Emotional Learning Self-Assessment			
Social Awareness			
	I don't think so	*I'm working on it*	*I'm good at it*
I can understand why someone else thinks or feels differently than me.			
I understand that people are different, and I like to learn about those differences.			
I respect others by being polite and listening to them.			
Responsible Decision-Making			
	I don't think so	*I'm working on it*	*I'm good at it*
I can figure out what the problem is when I'm struggling.			
I think about all the choices I can make, and make a decision based on is the best choice.			
I do the right thing, even when it's not easy, or what I want to do.			

Social-Emotional Learning Self-Assessment			
Self-Management			
	I don't think so	*I'm working on it*	*I'm good at it*
If I'm mad or upset, I stop and calm down before I do anything.			
I motivate myself to do things, even if I don't want to.			
I set goals and try to accomplish them.			
Relationship Skills			
	I don't think so	*I'm working on it*	*I'm good at it*
When I'm working with others, I can clearly explain what I'm thinking.			
Social-Emotional Learning Self-Assessment			
It's easy for me to make new friends.			
I work well with others when I'm working in a team or group.			

Growth Mindset

Growth mindset is another area that is important to consider. What a student believes about his or her potential for learning matters. If Ricardo believes that he can be successful with new concepts, especially if he puts forth effort, that growth mindset will help him be more likely to succeed. On the other hand, if Kelly thinks that you are either smart or you aren't, which is a fixed mindset, she is unlikely to try to learn new things, and she is less likely to succeed.

Understanding the growth mindset aspects for each student can help you differentiate their instruction. Using a series of statements, you can assess whether students have a strong or weak growth mindset, or a fixed mindset. For primary students, you will want to use the assessment orally, for elementary students, use the yes/no version below, and for middle and high school students, you can use the scaled version for your assessment as well as student self-assessment.

Elementary Growth Mindset Assessment	Yes	No
If you are smart, you don't have to try hard.	☺	☹
The harder you work, the smarter you will be.	☺	☹
I can learn new things, but it doesn't mean I'm smart; I'm just lucky.	☺	☹
Only some people are really good at certain subjects, like math.	☺	☹
If something is too hard, I give up because I'm not smart enough.	☺	☹
I like it when work is easy for me.	☺	☹

Elementary Growth Mindset Assessment

	Yes	No
I like learning when I have to think hard.	☺	☹
If someone gives me feedback about something I can improve, I get upset.	☺	☹
If I don't know what to do, that means I'm not smart enough.	☺	☹
I don't like trying new things, especially if they look hard.	☺	☹
I'll ask for help if I need it.	☺	☹

Middle/High School Growth Assessment

	Strongly Disagree	Disagree	I Don't Know	Agree	Strongly Agree
If you are smart, you don't have to try hard.					
The harder you work, the smarter you will be.					
I can learn new things, but it doesn't mean I'm smart; I'm just lucky.					

(Continued)

(Continued)

Middle/High School Growth Assessment					
	Strongly Disagree	*Disagree*	*I Don't Know*	*Agree*	*Strongly Agree*
Only some people are really good at certain subjects, like math.					
If something is too hard, I give up because I'm not smart enough.					
I like it when work is easy for me.					
I like learning when I have to think hard.					
If someone gives me feedback about something I can improve, I get upset.					
If I don't know what to do, that means I'm not smart enough.					
I don't like trying new things, especially if they look hard.					

Middle/High School Growth Assessment					
	Strongly Disagree	Disagree	I Don't Know	Agree	Strongly Agree
I'll ask for help if I need it.					

You may want to use the assessment multiple times during the year to gauge growth and changes.

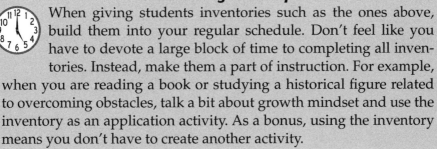

Time Management Tip

When giving students inventories such as the ones above, build them into your regular schedule. Don't feel like you have to devote a large block of time to completing all inventories. Instead, make them a part of instruction. For example, when you are reading a book or studying a historical figure related to overcoming obstacles, talk a bit about growth mindset and use the inventory as an application activity. As a bonus, using the inventory means you don't have to create another activity.

A Final Note

Building a portrait of each of your students is critical to differentiated instruction, because this information drives your decisions about what and how to differentiate. Build a complete portrait at the beginning of the year and update it throughout the year so it continues to be a useful tool.

Points to Ponder

The most important thing I learned was . . .
I was surprised about . . .
I want to learn more about . . .
I'd like to try . . .

3

Expectations

One aspect of differentiation is the content that is provided to students. In our model, that falls under the expectations you have for students. Although expectations are woven throughout the differentiation process, they begin with the goals and objectives we present to students, and the content used to achieve those goals and objectives.

Planning for Accomplishment of Rigorous Goals

There are a variety of ways to plan. When I was a first-year teacher, I simply looked through my resources, planned my lesson, and matched it to an objective. Then I wrote or adapted a test or project to measure what my students learned. Now I know that wasn't the best way. However, that process is still used in some classrooms for planning instruction and assessment. It doesn't necessarily ensure rigor.

An alternative I prefer is the Task Cycle. I researched this model from the DuPont Corporation while working on my doctorate. The Task Cycle focuses on starting with the rationale (or purpose) and desired result (product) before determining the process or resources needed.

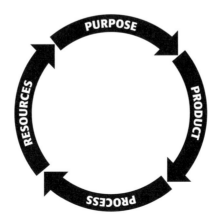

Think about how this applies to the classroom. Too often, we start with the process (how to get there) and resources (what we use to teach). For example, perhaps what I plan is for students to learn about Martin Luther King Jr. and the Civil Rights Movement by viewing (process) his "I Have a Dream" speech online (resource).

Let's turn that around with the Task Cycle. We want students to understand the impact Martin Luther King Jr. had on the Civil Rights movement (purpose), and we want students to demonstrate their understanding through a podcast (product). To do that, students will need to read about Martin Luther King Jr. and watch the "I Had a Dream" speech (process), using online news articles and the video (resources).

By starting with our purpose and product, which is the assessment, we can ensure a higher quality, more rigorous lesson. However, the model also applies to instruction, as you saw earlier.

Purpose (Expectations)

The first part of the Task Cycle is to decide on the purpose. The purpose will be embedded throughout all parts of the cycle. To determine the purpose, we need to clarify some vocabulary. There are several terms that are often used interchangeably, but they actually have different characteristics and areas of focus.

> Goals
> Standards
> Objectives
> Learning Targets

Goals are broad expectations for students, which can be for multiple grade levels and/or subjects. For example, "students will be lifelong learners" is a typical goal for schools. They may be embedded within our instruction and assessment, but are not necessarily specific to particular strategies and assessments.

Standards are usually content based and are limited to a grade level and grade range. Generally, standards are created at the national or state level and are intended to ensure all students learn the same content during a school year.

Objectives are narrower. Although some may be specific to a lesson, they generally encompass several lessons, perhaps within a unit of instruction. Objectives are designed to guide the teacher when developing instruction and assessment.

Learning targets differ from objectives in design and purpose. Rather than guiding instruction, they guide learning. As such, they are written from the student's point of view, using student-friendly language. Learning targets are typically written for individual lessons.

Why do these terms matter? Because you may create different assessments for goals and standards than for objectives and learning targets. Understanding them is part of planning for your purpose.

Let's return to the goal of "students becoming lifelong learners." How would you assess that? Perhaps through an anecdotal record of teacher notes related to student behavior that indicates a desire to learn beyond the school day. Or you might have students complete a self-assessment of indicators related to lifelong learning.

On the other hand, standards, objectives, and learning targets will call for different types of assessments. It is likely that standards include many objectives and learning targets. For example, the standard, "Develop an understanding of fractions (i.e., denominators 2, 3, 4, 6, 8, 10) as numbers" includes objectives such as "Students will demonstrate their understanding by representing fractions in various forms such as using a number line," which would translate into the following learning target: "I can represent fractions on a number line."

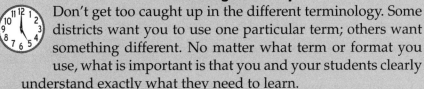

Time Management Tip

Don't get too caught up in the different terminology. Some districts want you to use one particular term; others want something different. No matter what term or format you use, what is important is that you and your students clearly understand exactly what they need to learn.

For our purposes in this chapter, let's look at a sample set of objectives, standards, and learning targets. We'll use these throughout our discussion of the Task Cycle.

Sample Standard

The student will design a map and calculate distances between multiple geographic points.

There are several questions that should guide your planning in order to ensure rigor for all students.

Questions

Did I match the essential knowledge and skills to the assessment?

Do students understand what to do and how it relates to the purpose?

Do I understand how well the students understand the goal, standard, objectives, or learning targets?

First, you must make sure that you start with rigorous goals, standards, objectives, and learning targets. Generally, with the national push for more rigorous standards, we have seen increased challenge and complexity in state and national standards. However, I've seen instances of teachers simplifying those standards into objectives and learning targets and, in the process, watering down the rigor.

How can you ensure that you are truly meeting your standards, etc.? First, look beyond the verbs in the standard. The verb only tells part of the story. A verb like "apply" can mean a basic application, or an application at a high level, depending on the context of the standard. As a part of setting rigorous learning goals, you'll want to measure them against a standard measure of rigor. We'll look at Webb's Depth of Knowledge (DOK), which can be used for this purpose, in more depth later in this chapter.

Time Management Tip

As I said earlier, no matter the terminology, your goal is for both you and your students to understand exactly what should be learned. It will streamline your planning if you make sure you fully understand the standard or objective. By spending additional time gaining a clear understanding of the essential skills your students need, you'll be able to more quickly make decisions on tiering, curriculum compacting, and creation of products.

Although we will discuss differentiated support, which is the "process" portion of the Task Cycle, in Chapter 4, and differentiated demonstration of learning, which is the "product" in the Task Cycle, in Chapter 5, I'd like to provide an overview in this chapter so you can see how you can use the same rigorous learning goals with all students while differentiating how students arrive at mastery of those goals.

Linking the Task Cycle to Differentiate

Product/Assessment

After you have determined your purpose, then you decide on the product. Because there are a variety of assessments to choose from, you'll want to make sure you plan the best type to match your purpose. Since we'll deal with specific assessments in Chapter 5, here we'll discuss general principles for choosing or developing a rigorous assessment as your product.

General Principles

Match the type of assessment to the purpose.

Incorporate rigor throughout the product.

Stay on track.

First, match the type of assessment you want to use with the purpose of the assessment. For example, if you want students to demonstrate knowledge of facts, the best assessment may be a multiple choice question or a short answer question that requires a list response. But if you want students to demonstrate problem-solving skills as well as an understanding of cross-pollination, a performance based assessment, such as the design and completion of an experiment, is appropriate. You may need to adjust what the product looks like, but all students should demonstrate understanding with these assessments.

Let's go back to the standards, objectives, and learning targets we detailed in the prior section. For those, there are several pertinent products.

Product(s)

1. Student-designed map with a minimum of four geographical features and a map scale.
2. Labeling of distances between points.
3. Conversion table to actual distances.

Next, incorporate rigor throughout the assessment. As we explore the different types of assessment throughout the book, I'll include specific recommendations for rigor for each type. For now, generally, you should:

♦ include a focus on higher order thinking skills;
♦ include problem-solving; and
♦ include justifications and explanations in responses.

Finally, be sure you don't get off track. Recently, I was assessing samples of student assignments in elementary, middle, and high schools. One consistent theme I discovered was that many assessments were very creative, but the academic work was not rigorous, nor did they match the goals, standards, objectives, or learning targets. I am a huge believer in creative, engaging activities, but if the assessment is focused on that, you can miss the academic piece. For the samples I evaluated, students spent the majority of their time on the artistic, creative side of the assignment, whether it was creating a flipbook or a Prezi. The assessments provided evidence of students' creativity, but less about their understanding of content. It's important to balance the two.

Process or Support for Learning

In the process part of the cycle, you work backwards from your product. Now that you know where you want to end up, you figure out how to get there. Planning how you teach a lesson is where your creativity can thrive! Think of all the ways you can engage your students, from pair-shares to hands-on activities to technology-based instruction. This is also a critical part of differentiation because support is where you will help each student, no matter where they are in the learning process, to be successful.

Sample Learning Activities

Students are given a variety of maps and asked to identify the geographical features using apps such as Google Earth or Kids World Maps.

With the same maps, students use the map scale to measure the distance between various geographical features in inches and centimeters, then convert those numbers to actual distances.

In groups, students use MapFab to create a map online. Students include a variety of geographical features, create a map scale, measure the distance between landforms in inches and centimeters, and then convert that to actual distances.

Individually, either on paper or online, students create a sample map with at least four geographical features and a map scale.

Individually, students measure the difference between the four points in inches and centimeters.

Students convert the inches and centimeters to the actual distance between places.

Sample Differentiation Support Activities

Advanced Learners	• After creating the map assigned to all students, find a country that has similar features. Compare and contrast the features and the distances measured.
Struggling Students	• Provide a basic outline of a map with four geographical features. • Provide a sample chart of how to convert the distance on a map to actual distance.

Time Management Tip

Notice how the process is tightly tied to the purpose. If you have a clear purpose, it allows you to focus your process.

Resources

The final part of the Task Cycle to consider is the resources needed. Although you can use the cycle to plan instruction, we will continue to focus on assessment. So, what resources do you need for the assessment itself? If it is a test, you need the test and an answer key. For a performance assessment, you will need the assignment and a rubric. For the products listed in the earlier section, students will need paper; pencil, pen, or markers; and a measurement tool.

Another Sample

Now that we've discussed the Task Cycle, let's look at how it applies to another standard.

Purpose

Standard	The student will develop a topic sentence and supporting sentences.
Objectives	The student will be able to identify a topic sentence and supporting sentences in a paragraph. The student will be able to describe the purpose of a topic sentence and supporting sentences. The student will be able to evaluate a topic sentence to ensure it represents the paragraph's main idea. The student will be able to evaluate supporting sentences to ensure they reinforce the paragraph's main idea. The student will be able to write a paragraph with a topic sentence and supporting sentences.

Learning Goals	I can identify a topic sentence and supporting sentences.
	I can explain the purpose of a topic sentence and supporting sentences.
	I can evaluate a topic sentence and describe whether the supporting sentences match the topic sentence.
	I can evaluate supporting sentences.
	I can write a paragraph with a topic sentence and supporting sentences.

Differentiated Process

General Activity: Using a "Know–Want to Know–How to Learn–Learned" (K-W-H-L) model, discuss what students already know about topic sentences and supporting sentences.

Alternative for Advanced Students: For those students who have already mastered the standard, provide them an alternative to write a paragraph using topic and supporting sentences. Have them work with a partner to identify topic and supporting sentences, and suggest any additional supporting sentences that could be added.

Alternative for Struggling Students: Provide a list of topics. Guide students through the process of creating a sentence about the topic.

General Activity: Using a read-aloud or other text selection, lead a discussion about topic and supporting sentences (incorporate pair-shares).

Alternative for Struggling Students: Reinforce concepts by using a second text, whether it is a read aloud, choral reading, or independent reading.

General Activity: Give small groups of students a text to read. Ask them to create their own matching game of topic and supporting sentences. Ask groups to swap cards and texts and play the game. Groups should then justify (either orally or in writing) their responses.

Alternative for Struggling Students: Play a group matching game of topic and supporting sentences that are provided to students.

Alternative for Advanced Students: Have students write their own text, and then create the game. They should justify their responses either orally or in writing.

(Continued)

(Continued)

Differentiated Products

1. Matching and sorting of game cards with topic sentences and supporting details (for all students; general creating with text, advanced creating own text and game, struggling using cards provided by teacher).
2. Short answers to questions of the explanation and purpose of topic sentences and supporting details (see number 1).
3. Description of whether a topic sentence matches the main idea, after reading a sample text.
4. Written text examples at end of lesson for all students.

Resources

- Game pieces and answer key for self-assessment.
- Short answer questions.
- Sample texts.
- Rubric for written texts.

Time Management Tip

 Use the checklist below to help you learn the process of the Task Cycle.

Checklist for Rigor

Purpose	Are the standards, objectives, and learning targets at a rigorous level (measured against an outside standard)?
Product	Does your product incorporate higher order thinking and is it at a Level 3 or higher on Webb's Depth of Knowledge? Are students provided an opportunity to demonstrate higher order learning even if they cannot work at the same level as advanced students?

Process	Does the process, or the differentiated support you provide for all students, lead to high levels of learning for all students? Is the support appropriate, or does it label or isolate some students?
Resources	Do you have appropriate resources for all levels of learners?

Ensuring Rigor in Your Expectations

Bloom's Taxonomy

Probably the most popular tool used to determine the level of rigor is Bloom's Taxonomy.

Levels of Bloom's Taxonomy

Remember

Understand

Apply

Analyze

Evaluate

Create

I think Bloom's is a good starting point, but I also find a challenge with this approach. We have come to associate Bloom's levels with specific verbs. However, verbs can be deceptive. For example, on the taxonomy, create is at the highest level. But is that always true? When conducting walkthroughs in a school, I observed a lesson in which students were creating get-well cards for a sick classmate. Is that rigorous? Of course not. The verb is deceptive.

Let's look at another example.

After studying Greek and Roman civilizations, students, create three-dimensional model to compare and contrast the two civilizations using only edible material.

Is that assignment rigorous? Students are asked to design a creative way to present their information. It seems challenging. After all, they have to be creative to complete the project. But if we take away the creative aspect, students are basically recalling information, which is at a low level of Bloom's. I believe we should provide opportunities for students to demonstrate their creative sides—but don't let that be a substitute for rigor.

Webb's Depth of Knowledge (DOK)

I prefer using Webb's Depth of Knowledge as a benchmark of rigor. Webb's DOK has four levels, focusing on depth and complexity.

Webb's Depth of Knowledge

Level One: Recall

Level Two: Skill/Concept

Level Three: Strategic Thinking

Level Four: Extended Thinking

As a side note, there is a very popular circle diagram of DOK on the Internet. It is a circle, divided into quarters; each quarter lists verbs for the level. Simplifying the DOK to verbs takes us back to the same problem as with Bloom's. Verbs can be deceptive.

When writing *Rigor in Your Classroom: A Toolkit for Teachers*, I contacted Dr. Webb's office to ask to reprint the wheel in my book. I received a quick and clear response. Dr. Webb did not create the DOK verb wheel, he does not endorse it, nor does he believe it represents the four dimensions. I understand why. The Depth of Knowledge levels are descriptors of depth and complexity that go far beyond simplistic verbs. Instead, let's look at a detailed description of the DOK levels for Math.

Summary Definitions of Depth of Knowledge (DOK) for Math

LEVEL 1	LEVEL 2	LEVEL 3	LEVEL 4
Requires students to recall or observe facts, definitions, and terms. Includes simple one-step procedures. Includes computing simple algorithms (e.g., sum, quotient). ***Examples:*** Recall or recognize a fact, term, or property. Represent in words, pictures, or symbols a math object or relationship. Perform a routine procedure, such as measuring. At higher grades, solve a quadratic equation or a system of two linear equations with two unknowns.	Requires students to make decisions on how to approach a problem. Requires students to compare, classify, organize, estimate, or order data. Often involves procedures with two or more steps. ***Examples:*** Specify and explain relationships between facts, terms, properties, or operations. Select procedure according to criteria and perform it. Use concepts to solve routine multiple-step problems.	Requires reasoning, planning, or use of evidence to solve a problem or algorithm. May involve an activity with more than one possible answer. Requires conjecture or restructuring of problems. Involves drawing conclusions from observations, citing evidence and developing logical arguments for concepts. Uses concepts to solve non-routine problems. ***Examples:*** Formulate original problem, given situation. Formulate mathematical model for complex situation. Produce a sound and valid mathematical argument. Devise an original proof. Critique a mathematical argument.	Requires complexity at least at the level of DOK 3 but also an extended time to complete the task. A project that requires extended time but repetitive or lower-DOK tasks is not at Level 4. Requires complex reasoning, planning, developing, and thinking. May require students to make several connections and apply one approach among many to solve the problem. May involve complex restructuring of data, establishing and evaluating criteria to solve problems. ***Examples:*** Apply a mathematical model to illuminate a problem, situation. Conduct a project that specifies a problem, identifies solution paths, solves the problem, and reports results. Design a mathematical model to inform and solve a practical or abstract situation.

Note: Descriptors for science and reading are available from webb align.org.
Credit line: Used with permission from WebbAlign © 2016. All rights reserved. WebbAlign offers alignment studies and professional development on Webb's Depth of Knowledge. Please contact us at contracts@wceps.org or 877–249–4211 for more information.

Do you see the deeper structure? It's more comprehensive, which provides a strong gauge of the rigor of an assignment. Notice that although Levels 1 and 2 are important, Levels 3 and 4 are considered rigorous.

> ### Time Management Tip
> If you haven't been using Webb's Depth of Knowledge, it may take some time to adjust. Most teachers find that the descriptors are common activities used in their classrooms (such as comparing and contrasting or justifying a statement or opinion)—they just may not be as rigorous as you thought. Don't rush it; incorporate the use of DOK over time.

Differentiating Content While Not Lowering Expectations

Tiering Instruction

Tiering, or providing differing, parallel tasks for students, can be used throughout all aspects of differentiation. However, effective tiering that ensures rigor for all students begins with expectations. Let's take a quick look at how tiering incorporates all aspects of rigorous differentiation.

Tiering and Rigorous Differentiation

Learning Portrait	Expectations	Support	Demonstration of Learning
Allows students to start where they are and grow to a higher level.	Parallel tasks at varied levels of depth and abstractness.	Various degrees of scaffolding and support.	Different activities related to same goal.

Diane Heacox, in *Differentiating Instruction in the Regular Classroom: How to Reach and Teach All Learners* (2002), lists seven ways to structure tiered assignments.

We will discuss strategies that can support tiering in Chapters 4 and 5, but at this point let's look at an overview of tiering related to expectations: What content are you going to provide, whether through curriculum, resources, activities, or support? And is that content rigorous?

Time Management Tip

Planning tiers takes a lot of work (and time), partly because it is basically planning multiple lessons, and because you are trying to adjust what you are doing based on the learning profiles. The tiered groups also change, rather than being constant, and that takes time. I start slowly. For my first readiness tiered lesson, I create the standard lesson, which includes an application. Then, I plan for a period of time (perhaps 30 minutes) where I develop an activity that is a higher level application for my advanced and gifted students to do instead of the standard application task. Finally, I plan how I can work with a small group that scaffolds instruction so they can complete the standard application. In other words, the "extra" planning is a higher level application activity, and scaffolding for my struggling students.

Tiered by Challenge Level, Complexity, Product, or Outcome

Probably the most common version of tiering, providing tasks that are differentiated by the level of challenge, is tailored to the readiness level of students. Closely tied to challenge is the level of complexity. Unfortunately, we often lower the level of the task for different groups, rather than adjusting the task while still allowing students to work at rigorous levels. At times, we do this by simplifying the product or outcome so much that some students are not challenged appropriately. Let's look at an example with a typical lesson.

Perhaps you are teaching proper fractions and mixed numbers in your math classroom. [Note: there is some variance among teachers as to the appropriate terms. For our example, we are using "proper fractions" for fractions in which the numerator is less than the denominator (such as 2/3 or 5/12), "improper fractions" for those that have a numerator equal to or greater than the denominator (such as 8/8 or 6/4), and "mixed numbers" for a combination of a whole number and a proper fraction (such as 1 2/3 or 6 5/12).] The sample lesson is not designed to be a complete lesson, but is simply an example of how tiering can be incorporated into instruction. Your objective is that students understand and apply mixed numbers. A typical lesson might begin with a review of proper fractions, such as 2/3, then continue with a discussion of improper fractions and mixed numbers, with examples of each. Next, students practice identifying the two types with a partner. Then they complete a worksheet for homework.

Let's adjust this to a basic lesson tiered by the level of challenge. After the review, discussion, and guided practice, students work on tiered tasks, either alone, with a partner, or in small groups. Note that tiers listed in the table below are not the same as tiers described in Response to Intervention.

Possible Tiered Activities for Sample Math Lesson

Tier One	Tier Two	Tier Three	Tier Four
Given lists of fractions, students circle the improper fractions.	Given a list of improper fractions, change them to mixed numbers.	Students solve a real-world problem that includes the use of mixed numbers.	Students create a real-world problem using mixed numbers.

Now, let's take a look at the tiering options through the lens of Webb's Depth of Knowledge. Remember that Level 3 is considered rigorous. Look at the math criteria for Levels 1, 2, and 3 below.

Tiers for Sample Math Lesson Using DOK Levels

Level 1	Level 2	Level 3
Are you asking a fact-based or basic recall question? Do students represent a math relationship in words, pictures, or symbols? Does the assessment require simply following a formula or basic instructions or computing simple algorithms?	Do students specify and explain the relationship between properties or variables? Do students select a math procedure according to criteria and perform it? Does it include basic application of material?	Are students proposing and evaluating solutions or recognizing and explaining misconceptions? Are students formulating an original problem given a situation or formulating a mathematical model for complex situations? Are students using concepts to solve non-routine problems?

Keep in mind that, even though we want to adjust the challenge and complexity, we also want to retain a level of rigor. How do our tiered tasks measure up?

Evaluating Tiered Activities in Sample Math Lesson Using DOK

Tiered Activity	Webb's Depth of Knowledge Level
Given lists of fractions, students circle the improper fractions.	Level 1: Do students **represent** a math relationship in words, pictures, or symbols?
Given a list of improper fractions, change them to mixed numbers.	Level 1: **Does the assessment require simply following** a formula or **basic instructions** or computing simple algorithms?

(Continued)

(Continued)

Tiered Activity	Webb's Depth of Knowledge Level
Students solve a real-world problem that includes the use of mixed numbers.	Level 1: Does the assessment require simply following a formula or basic instructions or **computing simple algorithms**?
Students create a real-world problem that uses mixed numbers.	Level 2: Does it include basic **application** of material?

You may be thinking that when students create a word problem, they are actually "formulating an original problem given a situation or formulating a mathematical model for complex situations." However, writing a word problem that includes mixed numbers is basic application. I am simply writing a new algorithm, just with words.

In this lesson, although we have differentiated by level of challenge and/or complexity, none of our tiers included rigorous tasks. Let's turn our attention to tiered tasks that are rigorous.

The teacher starts with activating prior knowledge and a review of proper fractions, such as 2/3, and then continues with a discussion of mixed numbers (1 1/3), providing examples of each type of fraction. Next, students briefly practice identifying the two types by circling them in a list of fractions. Some students work alone, others work with a partner, and the teacher may pull a small group for extra instruction. After they have completed this activity, students generate a T-chart of proper fractions and mixed numbers. Some students are given a list of fractions to categorize on the chart; others generate their own. Although these are Level 1 activities, they are likely necessary for students to move forward. Minimal tiering was used in this part of the lesson.

The teacher then shifts to solving problems using both proper fractions and mixed numbers. The teacher follows a process similar to the one described above.

Next, students are provided structured tiered tasks, building to rigorous tasks in the second activity.

Rigorous Tiered Activities for Sample Math Lesson

Tier One	Tier Two	Tier Three
Teacher works with small group to review whole class instruction, guiding them through the process of generating their own mixed numbers and solving simple algorithms. With guidance, students solve one simple word problem that uses proper fractions and mixed numbers.	Students work in pairs to apply the information by creating new algorithms using proper fractions and mixed numbers. They switch problems with a second pair and solve the problems. Next, each pair chooses an algorithm and uses it to create a word problem.	Students create word problems using proper fractions and mixed numbers. Problems must include multiple steps and require solving at least two algorithms. They switch problems with another person or pair and solve the problem.
With guidance, students are given two simple word problems that include proper fractions and mixed numbers. The problems include the solution. They identify which of the two word problems is not solved correctly and why. The small group is divided into two groups. With guidance from the teacher, each group creates their own set of two problems, one of which is not correct. They swap sets with the other group, who must follow the same process as above.	Students are provided a set of three word problems that include proper fractions and mixed numbers, which have been solved. They are told that one of the problems is incorrect. They are asked to identify which of the word problems is not solved correctly, solve the problem correctly, explain why the original problem was not correct, as well as describe their solution and why it is accurate. Next, students create their own set of two problems, one of which is not correct. They swap sets with another student, who must follow the same process as above.	Students are provided a set of four word problems that include proper fractions and mixed numbers, which have been solved. They are told that some of the solutions are incorrect, but the number is not specified. They are asked to identify each of the word problems not solved correctly, solve the problem correctly, explain why the original solution was not correct, and provide a written description of their solution and why it is accurate. Next, students create their own set of four problems, two of which are not correct. They swap sets with another student, who must follow the same process as above.

Notice that in the second round of tiering, all students are working at a rigorous level by "recognizing and explaining misconceptions," a Level 3 expectation in Webb's DOK. That is exemplified in different ways, but they all finish at Level 3.

Tiering by Activity, Process, and Resources

Another common approach to tiering is to change the activity, perhaps by adjusting the process, or amount of support, and the resources used. Once again, let's look at a sample lesson, both the standard version and a revised version. For this example, we will focus on reading and understanding informational text, such as an article.

In a typical lesson on reading an informational article, the teacher would activate prior knowledge to determine what students already know about the topic, which in this case is oceans. He or she might lead a short discussion on oceans, providing additional context for students.

Next, students are asked to read the article on oceans, which is written on grade level. For some students, the article is too easy, for some it is too difficult, and for others it is just right. This does not meet the needs of most students. Now, let's look at a revised lesson with tiering incorporated into the activity, with differing support, using different resources.

In a typical lesson on reading an informational article, the teacher would activate prior knowledge to determine what students already know about the topic, which in this case is oceans. For those students with advanced knowledge, they are asked to write a fact sheet with key information. Other students watch a short video about oceans to build their knowledge base.

Next, students will read the informational article provided. However, in order to build to rigor, there are two stages of reading, with two texts. The teacher rotates to assist each group as needed. In these tiers, students are working at Levels 1 and 2 of Webb's Depth of Knowledge.

Reading an Informational Article: Stages One and Two

Tier One	Tier Two	Tier Three
Stage One		
Students are given an article on the topic that is written at a lower reading level than the standard text. Using a detailed "Thinking Notes" (see next page), they read the text, with the teacher's assistance as needed.	Students read the grade level article. A standard "Thinking Notes" is provided that students can choose to use.	Students read an article on the same topic that is written at a higher level than the standard text.

Tier One	Tier Two	Tier Three
Next, they answer comprehension questions, which are provided in advance.	Next, they answer comprehension questions.	Next, they answer comprehension questions.
Stage Two		
Students read the grade level article. While reading the lower level text, students have built vocabulary and background knowledge, ensuring they are more successful with the grade level text. Using a detailed "Thinking Notes" (see below), they read the text, with the teacher's assistance as needed. Next, they answer comprehension questions, which include opportunities to compare and contrast information.	Students read a second article, one that is written at a higher level. A standard "Thinking Notes" is provided if they need it. Next, they answer comprehension questions, which include opportunities to compare and contrast information.	Students read a complementary article on the same topic that is written at a higher level than the standard text. Next, they answer comprehension questions, which include opportunities to compare and contrast information.

What Are Thinking Notes?

Also called a Guide-o-Rama, a "Thinking Notes" is an enhanced study guide. In addition to providing outline points or questions, it includes "think-alouds," comments and questions to help students process their thinking. In essence, the Thinking Notes model the strategies you want students to use while they are reading.

Sample "Think-Aloud" Comments and Questions

"Before I start reading, I write down all the headings. When I finish, I have an outline and an overview of what I will be reading."

"When I get to a word I don't know, I use tools to help me determine what it means. I read the sentence before and after to see if it helps; I look in the margin or glossary for a definition, or I see if there is a table or chart that might help. If that doesn't help, I ask another student before going to the teacher for assistance."

"One thing that is tricky about reading an article is the maps, charts, or graphs. I was reading a paragraph one day, and it referenced a chart, but there wasn't one. I kept reading, and when I turned the page, I found it. I didn't think about the fact that it might be on a different page."

Students then regroup for a whole class discussion of oceans, which includes questions specific to all articles. This ensures that all students have an opportunity to participate, no matter the tier. These questions focus on comprehension, but the discussion begins to incorporate DOK Level 3 questions, such as asking students to connect information they learned to their real-life experiences. They are also asked to justify their earlier responses, explaining why they answered the way they did.

Sample Criteria for Webb's DOK Level 3

Do students go beyond the text information while demonstrating they understand the text?

Are students encouraged to explain, generalize, or connect ideas?

Do students identify research questions and design investigations for a scientific problem?

Do students analyze how changes have affected people and places?

Is there more than one possible response?

Are students required to explain or justify their response?

Do students evaluate the credibility of a message?

The teacher then guides students to discuss current issues related to oceans, such as pollution or overfishing, and moves students into tiers based on their understanding of the lesson.

Reading an Informational Article

Tier One	Tier Two	Tier Three
Students choose one of the identified issues related to oceans. Appropriate resources are provided. With the teacher's guidance, they create a three-column chart with the headings of: Issue, How Changes Have Affected People, and How I Would Address the Situation. Students would write a narrative explaining how the issue is impacting oceans, including justification for their points. They may also propose a solution for the issue, with details.	Students may work individually or in pairs. After choosing an issue related to oceans, students research the topic in more depth. They find at least two sources, one of which is an editorial, website, or promotional materials for an advocacy group, or some other type of opinion about the issue. Next, they evaluate the credibility of their opinion piece, comparing it to the factual information found in other sources. Finally, they write a critique of the editorial, website, or promotional materials, or other type of opinion. The critique should include their opinion as well as a justification of their points, which includes factual information. They conclude with their own opinion as to a solution as well as an explanation of it.	Students choose an issue, either one identified in class or another one based on their research (a minimum of three appropriate sources). Individually, students create a research question, describe an appropriate investigation approach, and justify why their investigation needs to occur and how it will impact society.

Notice that, although different activities, resources, and support were provided, each student concluded their work by completing a rigorous activity.

Compacting Curriculum

One particular concern that drives differentiated learning is the lack of rigor for students who are gifted and talented. That has since been widened to include advanced students, who may not be identified as gifted and talented. Too often, students who are working at a more advanced stage have already mastered the current content. Because they are not held to rigorous expectations, they are bored, which often leads to disengagement and underachievement. If we want to increase rigor for all students, differentiating for advanced students is particularly important.

One strategy that has been shown to be effective is curriculum compacting, which was developed by Joe Renzulli at the University of Connecticut and is specifically designed to help advanced learners maximize their use of time for learning (Reis, Renzulli, & Burns, 2016). Compacting is a three-stage process.

Stage 1: The teacher identifies students who are candidates for compacting and assesses what they know and do not know about a particular topic or chapter.

Stage 2: The teacher notes any skills or understandings covered in the study in which the student did not demonstrate mastery, and then lays out a plan to make certain the student learns those things.

Stage 3: The teacher and student design an investigation or study for the student to engage in while others are working with the general lessons. Students then complete the investigation or study.

Stage 1 is the pre-assessment process, which is critical to compacting. You can use a variety of tools to determine what content students have already mastered, from pre-tests to interviews, but it is important to ensure that the assessment reflects mastery. We discussed some assessments in Chapter 2, and we will also look at additional ones in Chapter 5. You may want to refer to those sections when using curriculum compacting. However, there are three general guidelines to consider that are essential elements of effective pre-assessments for compacting.

Time Management Tips

There will be multiple times throughout the book that I will recommend you work with other teachers to save time. Creating or finding a pre-assessment is definitely a time to share the workload. Rotating who is responsible for the pre-assessment shares the workload and saves you time overall.

Once you have identified students eligible for compacting, then you will plan your instruction. Dr. Renzulli and Linda Smith created "The Compactor" for this purpose. Follow the three steps on the next page to plan students' instruction.

Time Management Tip

The compacting tool is helpful, and it's structured quite well. You are actually following a three-step process. First, identify what needs to be compacted. Next, list how you will have students show they have mastered the standard content, and then plan your enrichment activities. I'd combine the last two to simplify the planning. Create enrichment activities that include demonstrating understanding of the standard content. For example, in a middle school math classroom, while teaching Pascal's Triangle, the enrichment activity is for students to design and create a real-life item that uses Pascal's Triangle. Then, students write a reflection justifying how the item incorporates all aspects of Pascal's Triangle. Even if they are able to create the item without understanding all the details of Pascal's Triangle, they definitely must show they understand the detail while writing the reflection.

INDIVIDUAL EDUCATIONAL PROGRAMMING GUIDE
The Compactor

Prepared by: Joseph S. Renzulli
Linda M. Smith

NAME _____ AGE _____ TEACHER(S) _____

Individual Conference Dates And Persons
Participating in Planning Of IEP

SCHOOL _____ GRADE _____ PARENT(S) _____

CURRICULUM AREAS TO BE CONSIDERED FOR COMPACTING Provide a brief description of basic material to be covered during this marking period and the assessment information or evidence that suggests the need for compacting.	PROCEDURES FOR COMPACTING BASIC MATERIAL Describe activities that will be used to guarantee proficiency in basic curricular areas.	ACCELERATION AND/OR ENRICHMENT ACTIVITIES Describe activities that will be used to provide advanced level learning experiences in each area of the regular curriculum.

☐ Check here if additional information is recorded on the reverse side.

Smith and Throne (2010) provide us an example of a lesson that includes compacting for two students.

Let's say your class is about to begin a study of the solar system. One week prior to starting this unit, ask each student to use a KWL chart to list what he/she already knows about this topic in the "K" column of his/her chart. Also ask your students to write their questions in the "W" column, which asks what they wonder about the solar system. As you review the responses, you may find that two students' KWL charts indicate mastery of the content, as outlined in the unit's objectives. On their charts, the students accurately named and described the planets, and shared other interesting facts about comets, asteroids, meteors, etc. It is obvious that these students already know the content the class is about to investigate, so you may decide to compact the curriculum on the solar system for these two. Instead of studying what they already know, let them extend their learning on a specific topic that relates to the solar system. This way they can apply the facts they know to a meaningful project. Then they might meet with your teacher-directed group only when a lesson is offered on a topic they have not yet mastered.

♦ To begin, meet with the two students to identify an area of interest that aligns with the unit's objectives. Have them use the Extension Activity Menu to choose a project that will demonstrate their learning. Say the students choose "building a model" from the list and choose to study the size of each planet relative to that of the sun. They decide to begin by building a miniature model of the sun (100 mm in diameter), which will serve as the point of reference for the entire solar system.

♦ Each planet's size will be based on that of the model of the sun.

♦ Next, review the Compacting Contract with the students. Make sure the topic, the product, the rules, and a rubric are listed and agreed upon. With the solar system for their model, let's say the students use the following criteria to evaluate their project:

   ♦ The objective is to create a mathematically accurate miniature model of the solar system that shows the size of each planet relative to that of the sun.

   ♦ The following percentages will serve as the rubric's criteria for success: 4 = 90–100% accuracy; 3 = 80–89% accuracy; 2 = 70–79% accuracy; 1 = below 70% accuracy

♦ When the model is complete, the students decide how and to whom to present it. The relative size of the sun and the planets is measured and shared by the students. After the presentation, you enter the information on each student's Compacting Record sheet.

This example shows how the teacher, in addition to increasing the rigor for the two students, also builds on the existing objectives, rather than changing the objectives. He or she also shifts ownership to students by collaborating with them to identify their interests, and then allowing them to choose how they want to demonstrate their learning.

It is also helpful to use a compacting agreement with students to ensure clarity and provide accountability.

Compacting Agreement

Name: *Quanterria*   Subject: *English*

Unit: *Mythology*

Beginning Date: *October 15*   Completion Date: *November 5*

Reason for Compacting: *Preassessment indicates mastery of the topic: names of the major Greek mythological figures, their attributes, and their roles.*

Assignment: *Conduct research using multiple sources (from the school library, public library, and the Internet) and write a 5–10 page paper on the influence of Greek mythology on the culture, arts, and literature of Western civilization.*

Final Product(s): *5–10 page paper*

Evaluation Criteria: *Rubric for research papers*

Student's Signature: *Quanterria*   Date: *October 15*

Teacher's Signature: *Mr. Sykes*   Date: *October 15*

Source: https://iris.peabody.vanderbilt.edu/wp-content/uploads/modules/di/pdfs/di_05_link_compact_done.pdf#content

Time Management Tip
Use a template for the compacting that can be easily completed. For example, using a word template, all I have to do is change the dates, etc. I also like an alternative for the form,

using a simple process. Give older students a half-page sheet of paper labeled "What I Already Know," which they complete based on their pre-assessment. They sign that they understand and will complete the task. Next, give students the instruction for their assignment in writing, along with any rubrics or supporting materials, and the deadline for completion. This is a streamlined process that retains the main concepts of the agreement.

Curriculum compacting is not effective for all students. You may have an advanced student who is unable or unwilling to work independently. In that case, you may need to find an alternative strategy. However, compacting has been shown to increase learning for many students who are not challenged in their classrooms. It is one tool in your toolkit for differentiation.

Time Management Tip

You may not use compacting with every unit, especially when you are at the beginning stages of rigorous differentiation. Use it for one unit, reflect and adjust your process, then try it again. I worked with one school that set a goal of compacting once every grading period to allow teachers and students to become familiar with the process.

A Final Note

Having high expectations for students is foundational to ensuring rigor in a differentiated classroom. Although we sometimes think this is limited to the curriculum we present, it actually starts with the goals or objectives and planning for that to ensure all students master them. Then we can use strategies such as tiering and curriculum compacting to help students achieve at high levels.

Points to Ponder

The most important thing I learned was . . .
I was surprised about . . .
I want to learn more about . . .
I'd like to try . . .

4

Differentiating Instructional Support to Increase Rigor

The second part of rigor is the instructional support provided to students, or the process used to help students succeed in a differentiated classroom. Decisions about the types of support to provide to students will be based on their learning portraits, which we discussed in Chapter 2, and on the formative assessment you will use throughout the scaffolding. In this chapter, we will focus on instructional strategies to support students, and we will discuss formative assessment in Chapter 5.

Bicycle Model

When I was a young girl, I wanted to ride a bike. However, I had to start with a tricycle. I needed to be close to the ground, and I needed the support of extra wheels. However, after a couple of years, I was ready to ride a children's bicycle. Of course, it had training wheels, because I still needed the balance of two additional wheels at the back. I remember the day my father took off the training wheels so I could ride without them. He still held on to the back of the seat, to make sure I learned how to keep my balance without the extra wheels. Finally, he let go of the seat and let me ride by myself, one of the proudest days of my young life.

That's one way to think of scaffolding and support. Some students are ready to ride the bike right now. Other students may need strong, consistent support so they don't falter. Then, we lessen the support a bit, but still ensure that we have built in the scaffolding strategies. Next, we pull back a bit, but still stay close by to make sure they are successful. You'll want to differentiate how long, and how much, support they need. Lastly, they'll try it by themselves and show they understand the concept without your help.

Approaches to Support

There are two approaches to support: general and differentiated. General support is that which you provide to your entire class to help them be successful. Differentiated support, which can be in a small group setting or for an individual, focuses on particular students.

General Support

General support is critical, because in a rigorous classroom, students are expected to work at ever-increasing levels of challenge. As the rigor increases, so does the need for support.

In order to determine whether general support is needed, as well as what types of support will be helpful, you'll want to look for patterns in your pre-assessment and formative assessments. For example, imagine you are beginning a physical science unit of laws of motion, force, speed, and the transfer of energy. After using an anticipatory guide for pre-assessment (see Chapter 2), you determine that, although your students understand basic concepts of motion, force, and speed, no students demonstrate mastery of the transfer of energy. In this case, you will need to use the support strategies in this chapter for general scaffolding.

Time Management Tip

I used 5–7 general strategies that were useful anytime I was introducing a new concept or something particularly rigorous. These included graphic organizers, modeling of "what good looks like" for tasks, and chunking information. These were effective, and I didn't need to come up with a new strategy for each lesson. This allowed me to spend a little more time planning the support needed for my struggling students.

Differentiated Support

Based on the pre-assessment, you determine that you need to lead a quick review of motion, force, and speed so that you can address transfer of energy. During the lesson, you observe that some students understand the basic information, but they cannot apply the material or connect it to the real world.

At this point, you will need to address students' needs through differentiated assessment. This might occur in a small group or individually.

Only you can determine the best option, based on your observations of your students' needs.

Many teachers begin with small groups because it is likely the identified students are struggling in a similar manner. With focused instruction, students are more likely to be successful with the main content when they return to the whole-class setting.

Depending on the formative assessment used in the small group, you will then make one of three decisions. Once again, only you can make this decision based on your teacher judgment.

The student:

1. is ready to return to regular instruction at this time; or
2. needs additional small group support to return to regular instruction; or
3. needs individual instruction to return to regular instruction.

There are two important notes as you make grouping decisions. First, using the three options does not usually happen in a straight line. You will move students in and out of groupings throughout instruction. Second, small groups do not necessarily follow a "pull-out" model where a small group of students is regularly isolated from the class. Oftentimes, you will have all students in small groups you work with on a rotation basis, or you may choose to use learning centers for students.

Remember, the purpose of differentiated support is to provide needed scaffolding for students to be successful with your regular instruction. Although some students need varying levels of specialized attention, you don't want to create the perception of the "dumb group," a term my at-risk students used at times to refer to themselves. A positive focus on why students are in the group—for a bit of catch-up or reinforcement on their improvement—and the point that the goal is for them to return to the whole group instruction are critical.

Think about differentiated assessment this way. At the grocery store, there are three things that happen during checkout. Some customers go through the Express Lane because they have very few items they need. "Items" include the knowledge, understanding, and skills they need to go through the lane. The Express Lane is for your more advanced students. They have fewer items because they have already mastered many or all of the skills. The regular lane is for those who have more items, or more concepts or skills they need to understand to be successful. It will take longer to go through the line because they will need small group instruction to help them. Finally, there are times when the cashier calls the manager for an individual override on an item. These situations are for your students who need individual help. Everyone exits the store when they master the information, but at different times. In the classroom, all students are successful with the same content, just at different rates.

Determining Group Support

If . . .	Then . . .
You are introducing a particularly challenging concept or process that is new to students. This is likely a strategy that can be used in multiple learning situations.	Whole Group Support
Based on pre-assessment and/or formative assessment, you have multiple students who are struggling with similar issues. This may also occur when following common elements of Individualized Education Plans (IEP) for multiple students with special needs.	Small Group Support
Based on pre-assessment and/or formative assessment, and perhaps after small group support, you identify an individual who has specific needs that can only be met individually. This may also occur when following the Individualized Education Plan (IEP) for a student with special needs.	Individual Support

Time Management Tip

 Oftentimes, students who need individualized help are your students with special needs or students who are English Learners. Take advantage of the support of those specialized teachers; ask them for help either working with the students, or providing you material you can use.

Strategies for Support

Each of the strategies is useful in all of the types of grouping, perhaps with some modifications. Again, you'll need to determine which of these to use based on your pre-assessment and formative assessment. We'll look at seven strategies.

Seven Strategies for Differentiated Support

Encouraging a Growth Mindset

Adjustment in Instructional Style

Modeling

Text Support

Supporting Discussions

Graphic Organizers

Academic Vocabulary

Encouraging a Growth Mindset

Undergirding your efforts to scaffold learning for students is the need to help them understand they can learn and grow. Unfortunately, many of your students become so discouraged that they simply give up. You have probably seen this when you are teaching in a large group setting. When this occurs, you'll need to differentiate how you help students adjust their perspective so they can achieve success.

Time Management Tip
Don't get discouraged if this is a slow process. I've actually found that the least progress with the concept of growth mind-set is with my gifted and advanced students. They assume they are successful because of their ability (fixed mindset), so if they aren't successful, they are likely to give up, or not even attempt a task.

Emphasize Mastery and Learning
To help struggling students make progress, they will need to shift their focus from achievement ("I'll never get an A," "I can never finish this," "Everyone else is better than me") to an emphasis on what they are

learning. Particularly with older students, there is such a focus on "getting an A" that the joy of learning is lost. Some students are so scared they won't make a good grade, they give up before they start.

Ames and Ames (1990) made an interesting discovery about two secondary school math teachers.

> One teacher graded every homework assignment and counted homework as 30 percent of a student's final grade. The second teacher told students to spend a fixed amount of time on their homework (thirty minutes a night) and to bring questions to class about problems they could not complete. This teacher graded homework as satisfactory or unsatisfactory, gave students the opportunity to redo their assignments, and counted homework as 10 percent of their final grade.
>
> Although homework was a smaller part of the course grade, this second teacher was more successful in motivating students to turn in their homework. In the first class, some students gave up rather than risk low evaluations of their abilities. In the second class, students were not risking their self-worth each time they did their homework but rather were attempting to learn. Mistakes were viewed as acceptable and something to learn from.

As a result, the researchers recommended de-emphasizing grading by eliminating systems of credit points. They pointed out there were positive results from assigning ungraded written work. They also suggested teachers stress the personal satisfaction of doing assignments and help students measure their progress. This will certainly be a process that will take time for students to adjust, but the long-term benefits outweigh the obstacles.

Reinforce Effort

Encouraging and reinforcing effort are particularly important to build a growth mindset in your students. Students often do not understand the role effort plays in success. In *Classroom Instruction That Works*, Marzano, Pickering, and Pollock (2001) make two important comments regarding students' views about effort.

Research-Based Generalizations About Effort

♦ Not all students realize the importance of believing in effort.
♦ Students can learn to change their beliefs to an emphasis on effort.

Source: Marzano et al. (2001, p. 50)

This is positive news for teachers. First, we're not imagining it—students don't realize they need to exert effort. And second, we can help them change that belief. I think our words make a big difference in encouraging or discouraging effort. Claudia Mueller and Carol Dweck, researchers at Columbia University, found that when adults praise intelligence or ability in a student, that student will put forth less effort because the student assumes he or she already has the capability to do the work, so why try harder? This leads to a decrease in achievement.

On the other hand, when we reinforce effort, as in, "Wow, I can tell you worked hard on your science homework and it looks like it is making a difference," students will try harder, which leads to an increase in achievement.

Time Management Tip

There are mixed perspectives about extrinsic motivation. I definitely think you have to be careful about overuse, but I found in my classroom that using some outside motivators was helpful. To reinforce effort, sometimes I like using stickers or a certificate that celebrates that students tried. It's easier than always trying to take time to talk to a student while I'm doing other things.

Sample Certificate 1

𝕰xcellent 𝕰ffort

Excited about Trying Something New

There are also times when we think we are encouraging struggling students when we say things like:

> ◆ "It's all right. Maybe you're just one of those students who isn't good at math."
>
> ◆ "Bless your heart, you really mean well."
>
> ◆ "Don't worry about it. Boys usually make lower grades in writing."

Unfortunately, those comments send negative messages, especially to students who are struggling. They say, "I don't believe you can." When I was teaching, one of my students was identified as gifted. He was usually at the top of his group in terms of grades, was the first to raise his hand to answer a question, and always knew the right answer. However, when we started a new unit with some particularly challenging aspects, he struggled. I remember his mom told him, "That's okay; you are so good at everything else, this doesn't matter." She was promoting a fixed mindset. He was not good at this content, and he never would be. I was constantly encouraging him to put forth more effort so he would be more successful, but he gave up the moment she said that to him.

Provide Multiple Opportunities for Success

I believe strongly that students should have the opportunity to redo work they do not complete at a satisfactory level. This is particularly important as we want students to work at rigorous levels, and it is part of a differentiated classroom. At the primary grades, we use mastery learning, the concept that students continue to learn and demonstrate learning until we know they understand. If you are already doing this, I urge you to continue. But as students grow older, we tend to stop giving them multiple opportunities to show mastery.

The use of a "Not Yet" or "Incomplete" policy for projects and assignments shifts the emphasis to learning and allows students to revise and resubmit work until it is at an acceptable level. Requiring quality work, work that meets the teacher's expectations, lets students know that the priority is learning, not simple completion of an assignment. It also encourages a growth mindset. Teachers and parents often ask me, "But if they can turn it in late, then we aren't teaching responsibility. In the real-world, there are no do-overs."

I have found the opposite to be true. When a manager or owner invests the time and money to recruit and hire a worker, they do not immediately fire them for one mistake. Usually they give the worker instructions as to how to complete the task successfully, and they may even pair the worker with a mentor while he or she is learning the task. There is an understanding that not everyone is successful on the first try.

Additionally, there is real world accountability when I am required to complete my work. For instance, a teacher cannot just decide to "take a zero" rather than plan lessons for the next week. It is likely that his or her principal would insist on the completion of the plans. Most employers feel the same way. Requiring work to be completed at a satisfactory level demands that students prioritize completing the work and finding the time to meet with the teacher for additional support.

In my university classroom, I used a grading policy with a three-part scale: A, B, and Not Yet. If my graduate students were unable to complete a project at an acceptable level (B or above), then they received a Not Yet and revised their work. Originally, my students thought that meant I was easier on grading. The first night, I usually heard someone say, "Wow, this means the worst I can do is a B. That is great." For those students whose work was not at an acceptable level, I required them to meet with me and come up with a plan for revising the work. Then I set a deadline for the revision. It's at that point that my students realized the policy wasn't easy—it was more challenging.

Because they were all teachers, it was one of those moments when they learned more than content; they learned a process to use in their own classrooms. By the end of the semester, they had an entirely different attitude about learning and grading. As one of my students told me, "I didn't really like your 'Not Yet' policy, but then I realized you were teaching us to focus on learning, not on a grade. I'm going to try to do the same thing with my students." When you require students to finish an assignment at an acceptable level, you show them you believe they can successfully complete the work. If I returned to the classroom today, whether it was in elementary, middle, or high school, I would use this grading practice.

Time Management Tip

If you've never used a "Not Yet" grading policy, this is not the place to start. Because parents can be resistant, I try other strategies and build success before I change my grading. It's also helpful to do this along with other teachers, so you aren't on your own.

Another alternative is to provide a structured opportunity to improve learning. As Abbigail Armstrong, a former middle school teacher and a current university professor, graded a set of tests, answers to one particular question jumped out at her. The students had made significant mistakes, and clearly did not understand the content. She realized that she had not covered the material as well as she thought. Rather than simply failing everyone in the class, she looked for an alternative to ensure understanding. As a part of their mid-term exam, she required her students to complete a question in a take-home testing format. Using any course materials, they had to revisit the prior test question and correct or clarify any incorrect or incomplete information. They also identified new information they believed they should have included in their original essays.

There was a key benefit of this process: her students viewed the tests differently. As one stated, "You didn't just give me a grade; if you had, I would just know that my answer is incorrect but I wouldn't do anything about it." Another pointed out, "We had to look up the incorrect information ourselves, so we will remember." Her students took ownership of their learning. And, rather than simply restating the question on the second test, she reframed it in a way that encouraged depth of understanding.

> **Time Management Tip**
> Giving students an opportunity to redo missed items on a test is an easier first step with grading. Students can rework any missed items, and explain how they arrived at the new answer for partial credit.

Focus on the Positive

A final way to encourage growth mindset in your struggling students is to focus on the positive. Asking students to keep a "success journal," in which they log all their successes in learning, is a great option for students. Not only does this encourage students to reflect on their own progress, it allows students to chart their growth. They can write everything from "Today I learned . . ." to "I'm proud that I did . . ." to "Even though I made a mistake, I figured out the answer was . . ." Keeping a written journal also provides students a positive reminder of their successes when they are struggling.

I met a teacher in Arizona who used a different approach to reinforcing growth mindset in a positive manner. A math teacher, she created a "Magnificent Mistakes" bulletin board. Whenever a student made a mistake on a math problem, they worked with her and/or other students to identify the mistake and solve the problem correctly. Then, they were able to post both the mistake and the correct solution on the bulletin board. When that happened, all students cheered because that meant someone had learned from his or her mistakes.

Adjustment in Instructional Style

There are several approaches to teaching, and each has positive and negative aspects. It is likely that you use a mix of them throughout the year. In a differentiated classroom, not only will you want to vary these for all students, but they are helpful as you differentiate for small groups and individuals.

> **Time Management Tip**
> From the ideas below, choose one to start with, based on which one closely relates to what you are already doing. Beginning by adjusting what you are currently using is easier than trying something new. Then, choose another strategy and try it.

Divergent vs. Convergent Teaching

With a convergent approach to learning, also called a direct approach, the teacher uses very clear, structured lessons with practice that typically lead students to closed-ended questions. Examples of divergent activities include memorization and recall questions.

Divergent teaching and thinking, or exploratory learning, is the opposite, with a focus on discovery learning. In this method, students take the lead by playing creatively, investigating a topic or problem, or conducting an experiment. Convergent teaching is ideal for students who have a grasp on basic concepts and problem-solving skills, and are confident in their learning.

In terms of differentiation, struggling students may need to begin with a convergent approach and then move to divergent lessons. On the other hand, they are often more successful when they begin learning content from an interactive approach. As with all differentiated instruction, you'll use your pre-assessments and formative assessments to determine the best option.

Concrete, Representational, Abstract

Another method of instruction that is particularly helpful in math instruction is to consider students working through a concept at a concrete level, then a representational level, then the abstract level. Many teachers utilize this technique when teaching place value. Students begin working with place value blocks, then they move to drawings, then they finish with abstract problems.

I've found that, even though this is designed for math classrooms, it applies to other subject areas. For example, a graphic organizer is representational, which can lead to a student expressing abstract thinking. In a science classroom, students can learn about changes in states of matter by observing the difference between ice, water, and steam. They can then see a representational version, using a candle, by which students can see a solid candle, see the wax melting, and see it vaporizing through the wick. Finally, they can transfer this to the abstract level by creating their own example.

Modeling

Modeling provides students with a picture of what they should do, whether we are modeling our thinking, breaking down steps into smaller chunks, or showing models of acceptable work.

Modeling of Thinking

Think-alouds are a critical part of every teacher's repertoire. When you think aloud, you're simply verbally explaining what you are thinking. Many students simply have no idea of the processes used when learning new information. They see learning as the code that is unbreakable because they don't have the key. What we know as teachers is that there are multiple steps that go into any learning process and that one way to break that down for our students is by modeling our thinking.

Amy Williams describes how she thinks aloud for her students.

In reading, I use statements like, "I'm not sure I understood this word. But, the author is writing about _____, and the sentence right after says _____, so it must mean _____." or "When I first read this I thought that _____, but then I realized that _____ because _____."

When she teaches writing, she models her thinking during the revision process. "I showed students several drafts of a letter that I had written. We discussed the elements that changed, etc., and I walked them through my thought process as to why I changed/added information as I wrote."

Sometimes we assume everyone else would know how to talk through that process. Your strong students do that in their heads, but your struggling students do not understand it. That's why it's important to model your thinking for students.

There are times when you want students to take notes, or process reading, but there are some who are able to work independently. Another way to differentiate while still requiring students to complete rigorous work is by using "Thinking Notes." This is a written version of modeling your thinking. Think of it this way: you take a traditional study guide, which provides an outline and guiding questions, and then add statements that model your thinking.

Sample "Thinking Notes" Excerpt

Page 46: The first line in this section says the text will explain the five most common types of government. If all I write are the types, I don't understand what they mean. I usually use a chart to note the type of government, and what it means. I am going to use three columns for future information, and I also leave some extra space in case I want to add more material.

Page 49: Now, we are reading in more detail the characteristics of each type of government. If I skip this part, I won't really know what the governments are about. I'm going to go back to my chart and add more details.

Page 56: There is a chart on this page. It's easy to think that you can skip it. When I was a student I thought, "If it is important, they will put it inside the text." That's not true. Usually, a chart highlights important information. Look at the information and add to your chart.

Page 72: In the summary of this section, there is a list of countries that use each form of government. You probably wrote this down earlier, but if you didn't, go back and add it now.

Finally, I'm going to go back, reread my notes, and see if I have any questions for the teacher.

Time Management Tip

If you keep track of the types of thinking statements you make verbally with students, you can use many of these in the Thinking Guides.

You can move students to a higher level of independence by having students identify what you are thinking or doing. This allows them to shift from your direct instruction to a guided practice option, which can then build to independence.

What Did I Do?	*What Will You Do?*

Breaking Down Steps

For most of my students, note taking was a chore. They either wrote down everything I said or nothing at all, and I did not understand the problem. I thought they were either perfectionists who wanted to write down everything, or they were simply disengaged and did not want to take notes. For some of my students, neither was true. They were simply overwhelmed with the process of taking notes, whether from my instruction or a book.

I structured my lessons to allow me to work with small groups to teach them to use a basic note-taking format with two columns. On one side,

I provided an outline of the main topics I would teach, and students took notes about each point on the right. For more structure, I sometimes put the number of points they should have on the right side. For example, when I taught the symbols of North Carolina, the right side had 12 bullets, so they knew to listen for 12 symbols.

After I taught them the process, they were able to work with the whole class to take notes, although they used the structured format. Over time, I provided less structure, so they would learn to take notes on their own.

It's also important to chunk material when asking students to complete bigger projects. When Kendra Alston wants her middle school students to write a paper about media piracy, she starts with a 1-minute essay. Students are given an index card and 1 minute to write an essay about problems. Over a period of several weeks, she continues to do short writing assignments with her students that link together to form a larger essay. Her students don't see the big assignment as hard because they've done so much of the work one step at a time.

Many teachers use visuals to help their students remember steps in an activity. Desirae Remensnyder, for example, provides key information for her science students. "I have a reminder board in the back of my room that highlights the important items for each lab. I list the safety equipment needed, proper disposal methods, etc. We review the highlights before the lab, and the reminder board is right in front of them when they perform the lab."

Another way to use visual reinforcement is through the use of a color-coded timeline. This is particularly helpful when you are asking students to do a longer-term activity. My students struggled with activities that took longer than a day or two. They didn't seem to remember what we had done or how it fit into a bigger picture. One day, I put up a chart with color-coded steps and used a large arrow to pinpoint where we were in the process. It made a difference immediately, and they were more successful.

Time Management Tip

You can also ask students to help you break a task down into chunks. For example, introduce an assignment for students to create a video describing how a historical figure, such as Martin Luther King Jr., might handle a current situation, like Black Lives Matter. While describing the project, ask students what steps they should follow to complete the project, and list these so students can refer to it.

Modeling of Expectations/Product

A related issue for many students is that they don't know what "good" looks like. We ask students to complete an assignment, and then we are frustrated when the quality of work does not match our expectations as teachers. This leads us to question whether or not the student cares about doing the work or to wonder if the student tried at all. For many of our most frustrated, and frustrating, students, they simply don't know what to do, or how to do it, or they think that they are doing it right!

This often occurs when you ask students to answer questions that require more than just reciting facts, such as describing the causes of an event in history, persuading the reader of a position, or explaining the results of a science experiment. Each of these types of questions requires higher level thinking skills and applying all those facts they memorized. Some of your students may struggle with these types of questions or assignments. Or they may be challenged with complex reports or projects. Don't assume that it's because they don't want to or just aren't doing it. Many students simply don't know how to do this correctly.

I was successful with a process for understanding "what good looks like." There were times all of my students needed to work through the entire process; other times, I would introduce the first steps to the whole class, and then differentiate the later steps depending on students' needs. However, all students were asked to demonstrate rigorous learning by the end of the process.

First, in order to make performance expectations clear and explicit, we need to discuss the assignment with students.

"One of the tasks you're going to need to complete to be successful in my class is to answer essay questions appropriately. How many of you have written answers to essay questions before?" (Students respond.) "What did you have to do to make a good grade on them?" (Students respond. Typical answers include: needs to be at least three paragraphs, needs to be at least five sentences, everything needs to be spelled correctly.)

Second, explain your criteria for what makes a good answer, and state these in terms that are understandable to students.

Sample Teacher Expectations

1. Answer the question. Be on point and don't include information that isn't relevant.

2. Provide supporting details and examples for your statements. Writing is like a chair; the seat is your statement, and each supporting detail is a leg of the chair. If you only have one leg of the

---

> chair, it isn't very stable. In your writing, if you only write one example, the writing isn't as strong.
>
> 3. Have a good introduction and conclusion; start and finish well.
> 4. Don't make so many writing mistakes with grammar and spelling that I can't read your paper.

Next, discuss the difference between your expectations and their prior experience, clarifying misconceptions. For example, I've found most students equate length with quality, whereas most teachers are looking for depth of understanding, which may or may not be reflected by length. You don't have to tell your students they are wrong; merely explain that you want them to understand what they need to do to be successful in your class.

"You'll notice that my expectations are a little different than what you told me you did last year. Although you can't really answer my questions with just a sentence or two, I don't just count the number of words or sentences. I look at whether you actually answered the question, whether or not you gave at least three examples to support your answer, etc. I know this may be a little different, so let's see what that actually looks like."

Fourth, show a sample answer, either on the board, the overhead, or in a handout, and point out exactly how the sample meets your expectations. Then, give students another sample answer, preferably on a handout. Pair students and have them read the answer and decide whether or not it follows the guidelines. You might even have them grade it themselves, although I usually start just with satisfactory/not satisfactory rather than A, B, or C. Lead a whole-class discussion, going to each of your points and asking students to explain how the sample compares to each guideline. For some students, simply working through the process is enough. However, this is another opportunity for differentiation.

If needed, provide a second example to give students an opportunity to practice looking for "good." This may occur as a small group, in pairs, or individually. Explain that, as they write their own answers, they need to do the same things. If students are hung up on a particular misconception, such as always needing three paragraphs, give them a model that does that, but "needs work" in other ways so they can see the difference in criteria.

As our focus is to move students to independent application, then give them a question to answer. Use something simple; your focus in this lesson is on the process of writing a good answer rather than demonstrating they understand new content. Provide a writer's checklist of the guidelines to use as they complete their short essay. During the next lesson, or the next day, review the points with your students through an interactive discussion. As you go through each one, ask them to look at their own essays and check if they followed the standards. Have them physically check each guideline on the paper or the checklist. Then, pair them up again to check one another's papers while you move around the room monitoring their work. Finally, give them the chance to rewrite their answers before they turn them in to you for a grade.

Time Management Tip

Once students have completed a project, save or copy some samples so you will have them next year, rather than creating samples on your own. You might also ask other teachers if they have samples you can use. Remember, always take students' names off the samples.

Jessica Chastain uses technology to clarify her expectations for students' participation in their first student-led portfolio assessment conferences. As she explains,

> I taped a sample interview to give the students a good idea of what to expect. When the class viewed the sample interview, I would stop the video after each question, have the students repeat each question to me, and then they would write it down. The second time through we watched the whole interview with no interruptions. Then we discussed it. When I interviewed the students throughout the next week, they were prepared to share their work with me, offer me their opinions of their strengths and weaknesses, and we were able to set a goal for the next part of the year.

Since she knew this would be challenging for her students, she showed them a virtual example of the entire process, and she provided instruction to ensure their success.

Many of your students need to understand what is in your head. As one teacher told me, "Most students turn in their best idea of what we are looking for. Sometimes they really don't know what we are thinking, and it's our job to make sure they do know." That defines this strategy; support your students to higher levels of learning by making sure they actually understand what they are expected to do.

Text Support

Preparing Students to Read Different Types of Text

Oftentimes, we assume that, if students can read one type of text, such as fiction, they will also be able to read a persuasive issue and fully understand it. However, these are different types of texts, and they require different skills for understanding. For each, students need to understand the purpose of the text as well as specific strategies that can help them process it. Jamie Ledbetter, an ELL teacher, shares four types of text.

Four Types of Text

Type of Text	Description	Examples
Narrative	Usually fiction, tells a story, contains a theme.	Fables, myths, and legends, novels and short stories, historical fiction, plays, mysteries, poetry, science fiction.
Technical	Non-fiction, gives information to perform a task, contains specific terminology.	Brochures, classified ads, directions, floor plans, recipes, menus.
Expository	Non-fiction, explains or informs, focused on a topic, contains facts.	Biographies and autobiographies, reports, graphs and charts, brochures, newspaper and magazine articles.
Persuasive	Designed to persuade the reader of the author's opinion of an issue, may also address the opposing side.	Advertisements and commercials, debates, letters to the editor, editorials, movie reviews, political cartoons, political campaign information, speeches.

Note: It is important, especially with expository text, to teach the difference between facts that are true and those that are shaded to express an opinion. Also, be sure to include online examples of text as you are teaching the types.

Time Management Tip

Depending on your grade level and/or subject area, you may need to address differences in types of text. You can do them all at one time or focus on the ones that are most important. Teaching these to students takes some instructional time, but if they understand the differences, it makes instruction easier later.

Strategies for Pre-Reading

Once you teach students the varying types of text, you'll want to show them strategies that can help them understand each type. There are some general tips students can use before they read.

General Strategies to Use Before Reading Narrative or Fictional Texts

♦ Look at the cover picture for hints as to the content.

♦ Skim the text for pictures to give you clues as to what might happen.

♦ Skim for names of characters.

♦ Look to see if there are a lot of quotation marks; that shows you there will be a dialogue.

General Strategies to Use Before Reading Non-Fiction Texts

(Technical, Expository, and Persuasive)

♦ Look at or write down the headings and subheadings; they help you organize information.

♦ Find any graphs, tables, charts, pictures, or figures that help with understanding.

♦ Identify any words in bold face print or numbers (such as measurements in a recipe). They are important.

♦ Read the introduction and conclusion if there is one.

♦ Find the index and glossary.

Strategies to Be Used During Reading

Students also need support as they read the text. Teaching them specific actions to take will help them process the text during reading.

Strategies for Students to Use While They Are Reading

♦ Make note of important information. You can use a highlighter, sticky notes, or take notes on a piece of paper.

♦ Identify any questions you have. You can use a highlighter, sticky notes, or take notes on a piece of paper.

♦ Write down anything you identify as evidence for something the author said, or an explanation of a statement or opinion.

♦ In a math problem, recipe, or science experiment, find any important numbers.

♦ In non-fiction text, look for any questions and write them down. For example, in directions for a science experiment, you may see a question you are supposed to answer.

♦ With a sticky note or highlighter, identify the information in a table, chart, or figure that helps you understand the text.

♦ If a picture is helpful, write down why.

Note for Teachers: I recommend you use a form of color-coding or symbols to help students identify the different types of notes you want them to take.

Another option for supporting reading of text is the use of guided notes. With this, you simply provide a frame for students to use to take notes. While you may have students who need this in order to learn how to take notes, it is important to move them away from dependence by providing less structure over time.

Guided Notes

Cause/Effect, Logical Order, and Compare and Contrast

Two _____ are related as _____ and _____ if one brings about or _____ the other. The event that happens _____, is the _____. The event that happens _____, is the _____.

(Continued)

(Continued)

Cause/Effect Signal Words

Comparison
To point out what _____ or _____
things have in _____ is to make a _____.
Writers use _____ to make _____
and details _____ to readers.

Contrast
To _____ is to point out _____
between things. _____
_____
_____

We will discuss options for students to apply the information they learned from a text in Chapter 6. As I have said earlier, all of your students may need to learn what to do before and while they read, or some may come in with the ability to read and comprehend text at a high level. Others will need some level of support. You can choose which of these different students need.

> ### *Time Management Tip*
> Don't feel the need to use all these strategies with all students. That can be overwhelming and can also confuse students. Choose the one(s) you think are most helpful and teach them to all students. Then, revisit them as needed, or use them in your tiered groups as needed. Utilize other strategies when necessary.

Supporting Discussions

Discussions are a regular practice in classrooms. The class may read a text, watch a video, investigate a concept, or listen to a lecture, and then the teacher typically leads a conversation about the content. There are three key ways to differentiate discussions to support struggling learners without sacrificing rigor: ensuring all students have an opportunity to participate, offering question starters for focus, and providing guidance for student success.

Ensuring All Students Have an Opportunity to Participate

First, it's important to make sure that all students, particularly those that are struggling, participate in the discussion. Oftentimes, your advanced students will dominate the conversation, while struggling students simply listen or tune out on the conversation.

There are several ways to guarantee that all students are involved. It's important to move beyond calling on students who offer a response. There are a variety of standard strategies for calling on random students.

Ways to Ensure Teachers Call on a Variety of Students

◆ Use popsicle sticks, index cards, or clothespins with students' names to choose respondent.

◆ If desks are in rows, use index cards to choose the row number, then the seat number.

◆ Distribute number or symbol cards to students; draw from your duplicate set.

Even though those help vary the students who provide an answer, I have a concern. Typically, we ask the question, then call on a student. Using a random method does not allow me to differentiate the rigorous questions to particular students. I prefer to keep a list of students (or use a seating chart), call on the students I want, and check them off so I can be sure I am not calling on particular students too often. This also allows me to balance calling on boys and girls or students of different ethnicities.

One of my favorite ways to encourage all students to participate is to use a think-pair-share before taking answers from the whole group. Each student is guaranteed to participate. Additionally, because struggling students have the opportunity to discuss and practice their answer before sharing it with everyone, they are more likely to participate.

Offering Question Starters for Focus

Providing a focused question starter for students who need additional support is another tool to ensure student success. Some students are fine with open-ended questions such as "What do you think about this?" but others need more structure. In the samples provided below, you'll notice that, even though some begin with basic who, what, or when questions, the starter questions move beyond recall to answer more rigorous questions. When we differentiate our questions, we may need to start with a basic recall question for struggling students, but if we limit our struggling students to the easier questions, we are not holding them to rigorous standards. Note that all starter questions should be followed by, "How do you know?" "What is an example?" "What is your evidence?" or "How can you justify that?" in order to increase rigor.

Sample Question Starters

- Who do you know that might react the same way?
- Who do you know who has experienced something similar?
- When do you think this might happen again?
- When would you use this information or strategy in the future?
- What is a real-life situation in your life today that is similar to this?
- What is an opportunity to use this information or process in another class?
- Where is another place (city, county, region, state, country, continent) that faces a similar situation?
- Where might you experience this type of position?
- How would you use this information in your life or how would you apply this situation in the job you want in the future (college, community college, the military, or the workforce)?
- How do you think a historical event would be the same or different if it occurred today and how would it impact our society?

Time Management Tip

Although it's tempting to create your questions "on the fly" during discussions, it is helpful to plan some in advance to ensure that you challenge all students at rigorous levels. If you create them at the planning stage and actually write them into your lesson plans, you won't have to take extra time to go back and plan them later.

Graphic Organizers

Graphic organizers are commonly used in classrooms at all grade levels, and in most subject areas. Graphic organizers help students organize and store information, facilitate comprehension, and recognize patterns used in the learning process. This leads to an overall improvement in learning, and because students are provided this additional support, they can master more rigorous work.

How to Choose a Graphic Organizer

There are two challenges teachers face while utilizing graphic organizers. First, often we use too many graphic organizers, which overwhelms students. I visited one elementary teacher who showed me a cabinet of graphic organizers. She had a different one for every day of the year. You may need to use them that often, but, as with any strategy, if you use them too much, they are not as effective.

Next, there are times we misuse graphic organizers. In other words, we choose an organizer that does not match what we need students to process, or it is too complex for students to understand. It's particularly important that we consider the purpose of the graphic organizer in terms of how it will help students learn.

Characteristics of Effective Graphic Organizers

- Provide a visual way for students to organize information
- Help students understand and apply content
- Lead students through the process of learning
- Allow students to master more complex and rigorous work

Examples of Graphic Organizers

Let's look at a variety of graphic organizers you can use to differentiate instruction for your students. Although there are a wide range of graphic organizers available—you can simply search the Internet for your subject area—I want to show you two examples in different subject areas that focus on helping students work at more rigorous levels.

Fishbone

One graphic organizer that I found particularly helpful with writing was the fishbone. The fishbone graphic organizer is used to explore the aspects of a complex topic. It is particularly helpful if you have one single, complicated topic, and then need to detail more information on ideas, examples, or attributes. The fishbone helps students focus, monitor their comprehension, and organize information as they complete the organizer. It also helps them see gaps where they need to find more information.

Fishbone

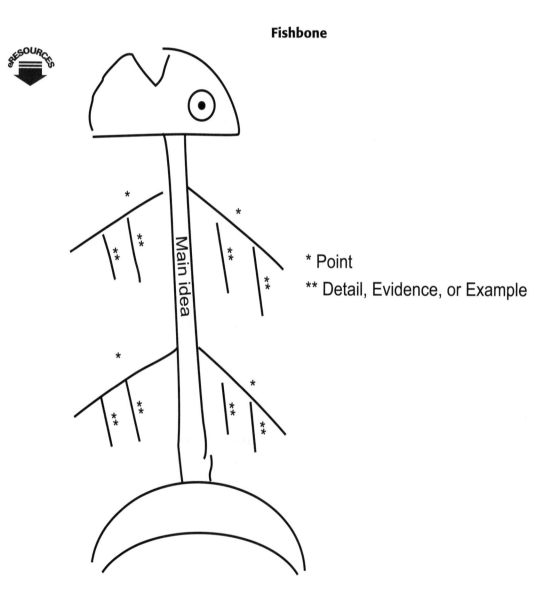

* Point

** Detail, Evidence, or Example

Flesh It Out

I originally discovered Flesh It Out while reading one of Janet Allen's books. She used the graphic organizer to teach characterization. After reading a story or novel, students would "flesh out" the skeleton with information, such as the character's thoughts (head) or something he or she said (mouth). I've found it to be a helpful tool when students are processing what they read or learn. Below, you will find two adaptations created by teachers in my workshops, one for social studies and one for math word problems.

Flesh it out

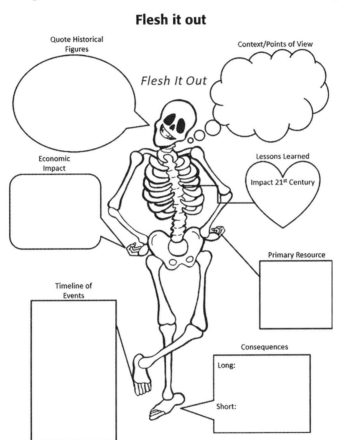

Thanks to Andrea Perdue, Tamikia Samuels, Brenda Blasco, Robin Collins, Kym Zamora, and Victoria Hunt for granting permission to use their work.

Time Management Tip

Simplify your choices. Find a few graphic organizers that will work with a variety of content. Also, don't feel like you have to create them on your own. There are graphic organizers on the Internet for just about everything you need. Alternatively, create one with other teachers.

Academic Vocabulary

When I was a student, the model for teaching vocabulary was simple. The teacher gave the class a list of words. We copied the words and definitions, and then wrote a sentence using each term. Finally, we took a test. This model provides routine for students, but it rarely leads to a deep comprehension of the meanings of concepts. One of my students just rearranged the words from a textbook definition and said it was her own. In a rigorous classroom, you are looking for your students to demonstrate they understand what a vocabulary word means, usually through an explanation with details, examples, and elaboration.

Students also tend to memorize what they wrote and simply restate it on the test. I remember when my nephew, Matthew, was in second grade. His teacher regularly used matching tests to measure whether they had mastered vocabulary. One night he called me very upset, telling me that he had a mean teacher. When I asked why, he said, "On this week's vocabulary test, she gave us words from last week. That's not fair. I didn't think I was supposed to remember them!" Isn't that how many of our students feel? We need to find a different approach to teaching vocabulary without lowering the rigor, as well as differentiating how we use these approaches for different groups of students.

Janet Allen's Vocabulary Organization

In *Tools for Teaching Academic Vocabulary*, Janet Allen organizes academic vocabulary by context. She explains there are four types of words: general academic words, domain- or discipline-specific terms, topic-specific vocabulary, and passage-critical words.

Four Types of Academic Vocabulary
General Academic Vocabulary

Domain- or Discipline-Specific Vocabulary

Topic Specific Vocabulary

Passage-Critical Vocabulary

First, there is general academic vocabulary, which is not discipline-specific. Students frequently see these words, such as *analyze, synthesize, contrast*, and *restate*. It's important to provide detailed instruction with lots of practice so that students are very familiar with them.

Next, she describes domain- or discipline-specific words, which are frequently used within a specific discipline, such as science or math. These words include terms such as *foreshadowing*, *hypothesis*, *rational number*, or *aerobic exercise*. Within the content area, these words should be reinforced regularly.

Third, there are topic-specific words. They are needed to understand a specific lesson or topic, and are typically critical to an understanding of the concept. Direct instruction is usually necessary with these terms. Examples include *Holocaust*, *biome*, and *impressionism*.

Finally, passage-critical words are those that are necessary to understand a specific text. These words are crucial to comprehension of the passage. Particularly for specialized words, direct instruction is needed. Janet explains that in the book *BATS: Biggest! Littlest!*, sample passage-critical words include *echolocation*, *horning*, *roost*, and *wingspan*.

You will find that, especially for those students who are overwhelmed with vocabulary, you'll want to put the most emphasis on general academic vocabulary and domain-specific words. These tend to be the most important for your content. It's not that you should ignore topic-specific and passage-specific words, but you may choose to spend less time on those concepts they do not use as often.

Another approach to classifying the words you want students to learn is to categorize your vocabulary concepts in a way that prioritizes those you know are most critical. In *Building Academic Vocabulary* (2005), Robert Marzano states that of the wealth of vocabulary terms embedded for each subject, some are critically important, some are useful but not critical, and others are interesting but not very useful. That is a helpful way to consider your vocabulary. Prioritize the terms and/or concepts that are critical for students to comprehend your content.

Prioritizing Vocabulary

Critical	Useful But Not Critical	Interesting But Not Very Useful

Once you have determined what vocabulary words and concepts are important for each student or group of students, then you need strategies that are helpful to build understanding.

Time Management Tip

Don't wait until it's time to teach a lesson to identify the critical vocabulary. Identify it during the planning process, which saves you time when revisiting lessons just prior to teaching.

Using Visuals to Enhance Understanding

Visuals can help students understand new concepts. I was in a social studies classroom in which the teacher was presenting geography terms such as *equator, latitude,* and *longitude.* She drew a circle on the board to illustrate the Earth, and then she wrote the word *equator* across the center. She wrote the word *latitude* horizontally from west to east where the latitude lines go across the Earth. Finally, she wrote the word *longitude* from north to south to clearly illustrate the meaning of the word. She provided visual context for her students as they encountered the terms for the first time.

Visual for Understanding a Vocabulary Term

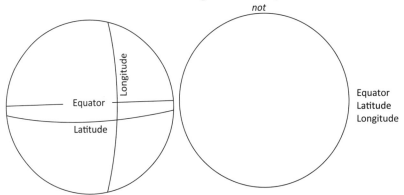

I used a graphic organizer to help students demonstrate their understanding in ways that required them to synthesize information about a term or concept and refine it down to the key points. Using a graphic organizer, students discuss different elements of a particular vocabulary term. I chose to discuss both examples and non-examples, in order to clarify misunderstandings. However, there are educators and researchers who believe that, by doing this, you are teaching misinformation. Whether you choose to discuss the non-examples should be based on your knowledge of students and your teacher judgment.

Vocabulary Chart

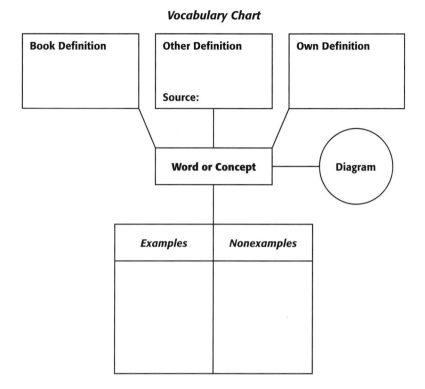

Then, my students could create their own graphic organizers to take notes about and demonstrate their understanding of vocabulary. I remember one student bringing me a graphic organizer she had created for the Pythagorean Theorem. She had used right triangles to organize the information. Using visuals helps students connect their learning.

Playing Games

We need to experience new words and concepts multiple times in a variety of ways. Too often, we expect students to fully understand a word after they have read it one time. However, reading a word multiple times doesn't ensure understanding either. Your students need to play with words in fun and different ways to help them learn.

During "Head Band," Erin writes a word on a sentence strip and makes it into a headband. First graders in her class give clues to the person wearing the headband, who must guess the word. All students are involved, and the activity encourages her students to learn from each other.

James Good, a middle school drama teacher, points out that his students find the language of Shakespearean plays challenging. For key scenes, students are broken into groups with five acting parts and a group director.

Students identify difficult turns of phrase or specific vocabulary words and make their best educated guess as to meaning. They run lines with one another to improve pronunciation and dramatic reading. The director makes suggestions as to simple stage movements that can be done in the small space at the front of the room. The group discusses appropriate tone, body language, and facial expression. Concerning themselves with the dramatic aspects of presenting to the other three groups more or less forces them to make meaning. Each group takes a turn in a kind of "drama slam." They try to outdo the others and get delightfully hammy.

Multiple Meaning Words

Particularly in specific content areas, it's important to teach words that have multiple meanings. I was observing a student teacher in a science classroom one day, and he asked, "Does anyone know what grounded means?" It was his opening question for a lesson on electricity. Immediately one student shouted out, "That's what happened to me last week when I made a C on my test!" Everyone laughed, but that's an excellent example of a multiple meaning word. We need to specifically teach students the different meanings of these words. Janet Allen shares a chart that helps.

Multiple Meaning Words

Word	In general, this means . . .	In math, this means . . .	Visual to help me understand
Base	bottom of something, support	number that is raised to a power in a mathematical expression	2^3

Time Management Tip

Once again, you don't need to do every strategy with every student. For example, if my lesson does contain confusing words with different meanings in different subject areas, I need to focus on that strategy. The games might be used during tiering.

A Final Note

A key aspect of differentiation is providing the support necessary for each student to succeed. By varying your groups, as well as adjusting the types of support you provide, you are able to start the process of differentiation while holding students to rigorous standards.

 Points to Ponder

The most important thing I learned was . . .
I was surprised about . . .
I want to learn more about . . .
I'd like to try . . .

5

Differentiating a Rigorous Demonstration of Learning

Another option for differentiation is to vary what students do to demonstrate their understanding of essential objectives. Of course, any of the varied options should be rigorous, as we explored in Chapter 4. Think about the relationship between product for demonstration of learning and rigor as a flowchart.

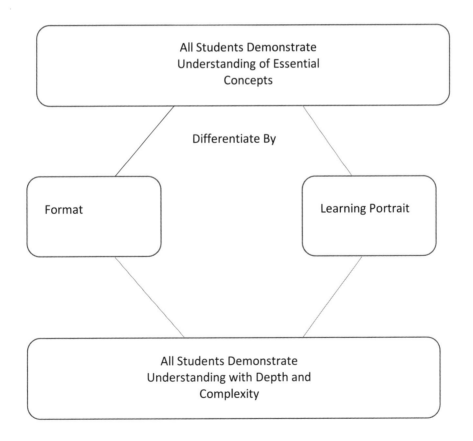

Since demonstration of understanding includes all of the tasks, assignments, assessments, projects, or tests we use with students, we need to consider what makes an overall quality assignment, then overlay criteria of rigor on the aspects of quality.

Quality Assignments

First, tasks, assignments, assessments, projects, or tests should be purposeful. As you think about in-class and out-of-class assignments, consider the standard(s) you are teaching, the type of thinking you want to see from students, and the ultimate product you would like. For example, you may want to prepare students for a multiple choice test. If so, some of your questions should be multiple choice. However, the questions should include applications and thinking questions, rather than just guessing questions about basic facts.

Time Management Tip
Although planning with other teachers is always helpful, making the initial decision as to the type of assessment is particularly beneficial. If desired, each teacher can still do their own version of the chosen assessment, or a group can create a common assessment.

The assignment should also yield quality results that show you the level of the student's understanding. In one of his high school classes, the son of a friend was given a list of words that would be used throughout the year. He was asked to memorize them, and was periodically given a matching quiz. Rather than simply asking students to memorize them, it would be more appropriate to introduce the words in context when they are relevant to the content. Then they could be part of the lesson, with a focus not only on the definition, but on the related concepts and possible examples and non-examples. Students could then write an extended response demonstrating understanding, create a riddle, or complete a graphic organizer (sample below). Each of these shows the depth of comprehension rather than recall. Which result do you prefer?

Characteristics of Rigorous Assessments

Of course, quality doesn't exist in a task, assignment, assessment, project, or test if it isn't rigorous. I was in one classroom where students were analyzing a diagram and drawing conclusions. While not as rigorous as

I would prefer for a summative assessment, I was stunned at the teacher's response to my question as to how she planned to increase the rigor. She said, "Oh, we already do that. Advanced students get to color the diagram when they are done since they can do more." Although we have discussed Webb's Depth of Knowledge in Chapter 4, I'd like to revisit it here, overlaying it to a set of criteria Rick Wormeli, in his books *Fair Isn't Always Equal* and *Differentiation From Planning to Practice*, describes rigorous assignments. Notice how these compare to Webb's DOK Level 3.

Wormeli's Criteria and Webb's Levels

Wormeli's Recommendation	*Webb's DOK Level*
Manipulate info, don't just echo it	3
Extend the concept to other subjects and topics	3
Integrate more than one subject or skill	3
Increase the number of variables that must be considered; incorporate more facets	3
Demonstrate higher level thinking	3
Use or apply content/skills in new or different situations	2 or 3
Make choices among several substantive ones	2 or 3
Work with advanced or primary resources	3
Add an unexpected element to the process or product	3
Reframe a topic under a new theme	3
Work independently	1, 2, or 3
Share the backstory to a topic	3

(Continued)

(Continued)

Wormeli's Recommendation	Webb's DOK Level
Identify the misconceptions	3
Identify the bias or prejudice	3
Negotiate the evaluative criteria	3
Deal with ambiguity and multiple meanings or steps	3
Use content/skills in real-world application	3
Analyze the action or object	2 or 3
Debate the merits of something taken for granted or commonly accepted by others	3
Synthesize two or more seemingly unrelated concepts or objects	3
Critique something using a set of standards	2 or 3
Consider and report on the ethical ramifications of a policy or act	3
Work with abstract concepts and models	3
Respond to open-ended situations	3
Increase expediency with a skill	1, 2, or 3
Identify big picture patterns or connections	3
Defend their work	3

Differentiated Options for Demonstrating Understanding

Differentiating students' demonstration of learning begins with the belief that all students will master the same essential skills, knowledge, and understanding. If we change the expectations for students, as we discussed in Chapter 4, we are lowering the level of rigor, particularly for struggling students. However, we can differentiate the products that demonstrate their understanding of those essential skills, knowledge, and understanding by format, and then differentiate the format by learning portrait (see Chapter 2).

Differentiating by Format

There are a variety of formats you can use with your students to ensure they have mastered content.

Rigorous Product Options

Tests

- Closed-Ended
- Open-Ended

Performance-Based

- General Tasks
- Tasks for Selected Enrichment Courses
- Project- and Problem-Based Learning
- Virtual Field Trips
- Scavenger Hunts
- Genius Hour
- Menus and Choice Boards

For each of the formats, we'll look at how to use it and how to ensure it is rigorous. At the end of each section, I'll provide suggestions as to how to choose or adjust the formats based on learning portraits.

Test Formats

Tests are commonly used in classrooms. Although there is much debate as to the effectiveness or rigor of tests, it really depends on how the tests are used. Certain types of tests measure understanding better, but all types can be used. It's easy to say that we are differentiating the level of tests by providing a standard multiple choice test as a standard assignment, a traditional matching or true-false test for struggling students because they are "simpler," and essay questions for more advanced learners. That is not necessarily true. A true-false test can be made more rigorous, and depending on the question, essay tests can be quite easy.

Below, we will discuss varying types of closed- and open-ended tests with recommendations for increasing rigor. Then, I'll provide suggestions for matching the type of test with different students based on learning portraits.

Time Management Tip
Don't feel like you have to create new tests from scratch. Start with improving your existing tests, and, as you can, create new ones if needed.

Closed-Ended Test Items

Closed-ended test items typically allow students to choose an answer from pre-determined options, such as picking True or False; a, b, c, d; or matching columns of items.

Time Management Tip
With matching tips, you might begin by simply adding a few questions that are more rigorous at the end of the test. Or, you might add 3 or 4 questions that are differentiated and assign particular questions to students. This is easier than creating multiple tests.

Closed-Ended Test Item Types

Type of Test	Characteristics	Increasing Rigor
Matching	Matching tests are an easy, quick way to assess a wide range of student knowledge. However, it is difficult to assess at a higher level of rigor, as most matching tests measure basic recall questions. Depending on the items, students can guess, rather than truly demonstrate understanding.	Make sure there is one best option for each item you list. Ensure that students can see why the items match, so that there is clear evidence students understand the link. Also, provide more examples than matching items. For example, if you have a list of vocabulary terms and then definitions, add one or two extra definitions to increase the rigor. You also might use a threecolumn matching test, rather than two- column one.
True-False	True-false tests are an excellent way for students to determine accuracy of a statement, agree with opinions, and define terms. As with matching items, they are graded quickly and easily, and students can answer a wide range of questions in a short amount of time. However, once again, questions are typically low level recall questions, and you may not be sure	Require students to rewrite any false choices as true statements, which does require them to demonstrate a true understanding of the content. In order to create effective true-false questions, it's important to avoid trivial statements and focus on core instructional content. Statements should be detailed enough that students must thoroughly read them, rather than glancing down to make a quick decision.

(Continued)

(Continued)

Type of Test	Characteristics	Increasing Rigor
	whether students understand the question or are simply guessing.	Also, if your statement includes an opinion, provide the source for clarity and correctness.
Multiple Choice	Multiple choice tests are probably the most used tests in classrooms across the nation. Although due in part to preparation for standardized tests, they are also easy to score. They also apply to a wide range of cognitive skills, including higher order thinking ones. Finally, incorrect answers, if written correctly, can help you diagnose a student's problem areas. Disadvantages include that the questions can't measure a student's ability to create or synthesize information, and that students can guess an answer.	Make the problem clear, and avoid repeating parts of your question in the answer. It's also important to avoid clues to the response in your question. Finally, although some recommend that you exclude the choices of "all of the above" and "none of the above," if you include those, it can increase the rigor, since students have to make multiple decisions about the quality of the responses.

Open-Ended Tests

Open-ended test items require students to respond to a prompt without any additional guidance. In essence, the choices are unlimited, based on what students know about the concept.

Open-Ended Test Item Types

Type of Test	Characteristics	Increasing Rigor
Short Answer	Short answer questions are an expanded form of fill-in-the-blank. Responses are not as long as essays, but they usually include more than one sentence. Because students are required to create a response, they are more rigorous than the types of items we've already discussed. Although more challenging to grade than matching, true-false, fill-in-the-blank, and multiple choice questions, they are simpler than assessing essay questions.	Build rigor into the context of your questions. In order to write quality short answer questions, be sure students know what they are expected to do. Keep reading level low, so that reading the question is not an obstacle to answering the questions. Finally, structure the question so that it requires a unique response.
Essay	Essay questions, which are sometimes considered a type of performance assessment, are one of the most common assessments used in today's classrooms. Essay questions are extremely effective for measuring complex learning. Opportunities for guessing are removed, so you can truly measure what students understand. There are several disadvantages, including the amount of time to grade them, the subjective nature of grading, and the dependency of the answer on the student's writing ability.	When you are writing essay questions, crafting the question is particularly important. You want to be sure the complexity of the learning outcome is reflected in a clear, focused manner. It's also important to provide explicit instructions as to your expectations.

Differentiating Closed- and Open-Ended Tests Based on Learning Portraits

There are two ways to differentiate both closed- and open-ended tests. First, you may vary the type of test you give to students. For example, based on readiness, I may give struggling students a true-false test where they are required to rewrite false statements as true. They still must show they understand the statement, but they are given choices, which provides scaffolding. On the other hand, I may use a short answer test for them as opposed to a longer essay test for my advanced students. My questions are all rigorous, and I'm requiring all students to demonstrate understanding, but I have varied the actual test they take.

Next, I can vary the tests themselves. For example, if I'm using a matching test, I might provide struggling students with a two-column chart to match, but I include more items in the second column to prevent guessing. As a step up, I can use a three-column test, which once again includes extra items in the second and third columns. I can continue to increase the rigor for my advanced students by asking them to create a fourth column on their own by identifying a related topic and listing appropriate choices.

Women's Historical Contributions

Person	Contribution	Time
A. Fannie Lou Hamer B. Shirley Chisolm C. Marie Curie D. Alice Paul	1. U.S. Civil Rights activist and wife of Martin Luther King Jr. 2. Ran for state senate on the platform of increasing minority employment. 3. First African-American congressman/woman. 4. Discovered the elements radium and polonium. 5. Formed the Congressional Union (later named the National Women's Party) to raise public awareness for women's rights as a part of the Women's Suffragist Movement. 6. Known as "Moses" and led many slaves to freedom along the "Underground Railroad."	7. 1800s 8. 1910s 9. 1920s 10. 1950s 11. 1960s 12. 1970s

For my advanced students, I can provide the three columns as described above, but they are required to identify a fourth heading and write information that matches each item in the original points underneath it.

Time Management Tip

You might start by using two columns, and having advanced students add the third column as described. Save the samples, and use them to adapt your test the following year.

With essay and/or short answer questions, I can easily vary the questions by interest without lessening the rigor. One aspect of rigor is making connections beyond the text, or what they learned. In each of these types of questions, I can require that students connect the content to a topic they value.

Open-Ended and Performance-Based Tasks and Projects

- General Tasks
- Tasks for Selected Enrichment Courses
- Project- and Problem-Based Learning
- Genius Hour
- Virtual Field Trips
- Choices

Universal Strategies to Differentiate Open-Ended and Performance-Based Tasks and Projects

Although we will discuss specific differentiation strategies based on students' learning portraits in each section, there are several options that are effective, no matter what format students are using.

General Options for Differentiating Formats

- Based on social-emotional learning skills, have students work alone, with a partner, or in small groups.
- Based on a student's culture, provide examples that are culturally relevant.
- Based on a student's special learning needs, provide tools such as noise-canceling headphones.
- For students coming from a background of poverty, provide additional support and experiences to build prior knowledge.

General Tasks

In a differentiated classroom, you'll want to incorporate a wide variety of formats students can use as products. Although we will discuss some specific strategies later in this chapter, it's helpful to start with ideas for choosing the best format as well as an overview of the wide variety of formats you can use with your students.

How to Choose the Best Format for Students' Products

1. Make sure it appropriately measures students' understandings.
2. Match it to students' readiness, if appropriate, but consider that each format can be made more rigorous or less so.
3. Match it to topics students value, if appropriate.
4. Remember that "cute" isn't necessarily rigorous.
5. Consider that options for students to "create" may also be simplistic (see more information below).

Time Management Tip

Because you will want to match some formats to students' interests throughout the year, consider having a "hotlist" of common topics of interests with students' names so you can arrange for products that allow students to match their interests and/or group students by interests.

No matter what format you choose, it should meet the criteria listed above. The number of options for products to demonstrate understanding is unlimited. Carol Ann Tomlinson, in her book *How to Differentiate Instruction in Academically Diverse Classrooms*, provides us a broad list of ideas.

Choreograph a dance

Write a song

Create an infograph

Conduct interviews

Participate in a debate

Produce a video

Develop a solution to a problem

Hold a mock trial

Create an object that reflects specific math concepts

Critique something

Formulate a theory

Design a game

Create a community plan

Ensuring Rigor, Despite the Format

Although providing options of formats, or types of product, is an essential concept of differentiation, one particular challenge is retaining the rigor of each way students demonstrate understanding. Let's look at several different tasks from Dr. Tomlinson's chart, along with a less rigorous and more rigorous example of each. The less rigorous examples are at Levels 1 and 2 of Webb's Depth of Knowledge. Please note that the more rigorous activities are not limited in their use for advanced students, nor are the less rigorous activities necessarily appropriate for those students who struggle.

Task Examples

Task/Format	*Less Rigorous*	*Explanation*	*More Rigorous*
Video Presentation (used in a variety of subjects; typically grades 4 and up)	Students research a topic using at least three sources. Then, they record a video interview to share the information, embed it within a	Despite the amount of time needed to complete the project, students are essentially summarizing information.	Students research a topic using at least three sources. After summarizing the information from each, students synthesize the information into three key statements. For each statement, students justify their statements

(Continued)

(Continued)

Task/Format	Less Rigorous	Explanation	More Rigorous
	PowerPoint slide presentation, and present it to the class.		with examples from their research. They also connect the information to real-life experiences that go beyond the text. Presentation format remains the same.
Oral answer to the question asked by the teacher (Primary K–2 Reading, but can be used with higher grade levels with upper elementary, middle, and high school reading, writing, and English)	Did you like how the story ended? Why or why not? What would you change?	Answers are strictly opinion-based and require an explanation but not justification from the test.	Make a new ending for the story that is related to your life in some way. Explain how the new ending changed the story, using specific examples.
Plan Design (Upper Elementary/ Early Middle School Geometry)	Draw a poster plan for a city. Detailed directions are provided, such as drawing six parallel lines, two transversal roads, a rectangular park of 24	Although extremely detailed and time-consuming, students are essentially either recalling knowledge (what is a parallel line) or applying the	

Task/Format	Less Rigorous	Explanation	More Rigorous
	inches with items like a round pond with a one inch diameter, and 13 buildings, such as two schools placed in alternate exterior angles and two buildings placed in supplementary angles.	knowledge of the concepts, such as supplementary angles.	
Web Page (can be used in a variety of grade levels and subject areas, typically grades 4 and up)	Complete the WebQuest on the history of the Aborigines in Australia, along with information about aboriginals today. Create a web page about what you learned, comparing and contrasting the two.	While it is both creative and possibly time-consuming, the instructions allow students to simply recall or summarize information, and compare and contrast.	Complete the WebQuest and the web page as described earlier. ADD: Learn about another indigenous population, such as Native Americans. How do you think the aborigines would react to a current situation facing the second population in a different country? Justify your response with specific examples.
Blog or Vlog/ Video Blog (can be used across subject areas and grade levels;	Students create a series of blog or vlog postings following each step of	The current task is focused on creating a log of steps followed to	Students create a series of blog or vlog postings following each step of the scientific process while completing

(Continued)

(Continued)

Task/Format	Less Rigorous	Explanation	More Rigorous
typically grades 4 and up, but can be used in K–3 as a class-wide project)	the scientific process while completing an experiment. The first entry should include a hypothesis and an overview of the experiment, while the final entry should provide an overall wrap-up of the investigation.	complete a science experiment. There is no justification of results.	an experiment. Initial postings should include an explanation of why the investigation is important to our lives today, pose the hypothesis, and provide an overview of the process. Throughout the experiment, entries should describe what is occurring, how (if at all) that step is supporting or negating the hypothesis, and what (if any) patterns are emerging at each step. The final entries should provide an overall wrap-up of the investigation, including how the results compared to the hypothesis, with justification for the response, recommendations for adapting the experiment for further investigation, and how the results impact real life.

As you can see from the examples, ensuring rigor is not simply choosing a format that may take more time; you can craft a rigorous or less rigorous task using most formats. For example, I saw the first activity with a video-embedded presentation used with advanced students. But that simply wasn't rigorous. As with all aspects of differentiation, you will need to be diligent about incorporating rigor for all students, not just those who are advanced.

Time Management Tip

Just like with the tests, don't try to create all new projects. Adapt ones you have, find ones other teachers have created that are available online, or share the work with other teachers in your school.

Differentiating Tasks and Products Based on Learning Portraits

Here is an example of the standard video presentation task with adaptations for both struggling and advanced students.

Video Presentation Task With Adaptations

Task	*Standard*	*For Struggling Students*	*For Advanced Students*
Video Presentation (used in a variety of subjects; typically grades 4 and up)	Students research a topic using at least three sources. After summarizing the information from each, students synthesize the information into three key statements. For each statement,	Students are provided a set of resources on a topic. Individually, in partners, or in small groups, students choose a source and summarize the information using a graphic organizer. After checking in with the teacher, students complete graphic organizers for two additional	Students research a topic using at least three sources. Students synthesize the information into patterns that link the topic with information from past lessons or other classes. If needed, students may complete additional research. For each pattern, students justify their

(Continued)

(Continued)

Task	Standard	For Struggling Students	For Advanced Students
	students justify their statements with examples from their research. They also connect the information to real-life experiences that go beyond the text. Students record a video, embed it in a PowerPoint presentation, and present to the class.	articles. With guidance from the teacher, students use highlighters to color code any information that is similar in the articles. They identify three key statements and provide examples from their research. With guidance, they also connect the information to real-life experiences that go beyond the text. Students record a video, embed it in a PowerPoint presentation, and present to the class.	statements with examples from their research. They also connect the information solving a real-life problem, and propose a solution to that problem using the research information. Students record a video, embed it in a PowerPoint presentation, and present to the class.

Demonstration of Learning in Enrichment Classes

Smith and Throne, in their book, *Differentiating Instruction With Technology in K–5 Classrooms* (2010), provide strategies for varying the product for art, music, foreign language, or physical education. As you review these options, reflect on how to incorporate these ideas without lessening rigor, and consider other ways you might adjust what your students do to demonstrate understanding.

Strategies for Varying Products in Enrichment Classes

Art	Music	Foreign Language	Physical Education
Restrict creation to pure imitation of another's technique or extend the liberty to create freely. Heighten or diminish the level of abstraction. Expand or reduce the levels of dimension, such as three dimensional versus one dimensional. Intensify or lessen the complexity or intricacy of pattern or shading. Add or eliminate the number or types of colors or textures employed.	Lengthen or shorten the composition or piece. Increase or decrease the number of instruments played. Increase or decrease the range of the piece. Modify the rhythm. Speed up or slow down the tempo. Heighten or lessen the dynamics. Allow for various types of parts or harmony: solo, duet, trio, quartet, whole ensemble or choir, and so forth. Include pieces of various classifications of music.	Increase or decrease the number of tenses used. Intensify or lessen the level of vocabulary. Communicate facts only or incorporate feelings and emotions. Vary the length or complexity of an exercise, document, or text. Incorporate simple or advanced realia and authentic documents. Invite recorded responses or spontaneous ones.	Intensify or lessen the level of competition. Increase or decrease the distance between performers. Require the use of the weaker limb, or permit the use of both limbs or the stronger limb. Change the levels of movement: stationary skills, tasks, or targets; moving tasks, skills, or targets. Add or eliminate defenders. Place or remove restrictions upon game play or technique.

My only caution with this list is that some items differentiate by quantity, such as using more or less of something. While that, at times, is appropriate, an overreliance on quantity can actually disguise the rigor of the task. Ten low level questions are not as rigorous as one that requires analysis and justification.

Projects, Project-Based Learning, and Problem-Based Learning

Do you remember doing projects when you were a student? I do. My teachers typically assigned everyone a standard project; we completed them and turned them in and then received a grade. It wasn't very rigorous. Today, teachers use standard projects, project-based learning, and problem-based learning. Let's look at how they compare.

Explanation of Three Types

Projects	Project-Based Learning	Problem-Based Learning
Finished product is the focus. Teacher works mainly after the project is complete. Based on directions and are done "like last year." Are oftentimes done at home (hopefully independently by the student). Are closed; every project has the same goal (such as create a diorama of the Alamo).	Student involvement is the focus. Teacher works mainly before the project starts, although some support is provided to students who need it. Are relevant to students' lives or future lives. Are based on driving questions developed by the teacher that encompass the learning and establish the need to know. Are open-ended; students make choices that determine the outcome and path of the research (such as design a fortification that would take your community through a bio-attack).	Student inquiry is the focus. Are based on driving questions developed by students. Are open-ended; students make choices that determine the outcome and path of the research. Project is student-directed, with the teacher providing support as needed, but typically in a guidance role.

Adapted from a blog entry by Terry Heick at teachthought.com.

Examples of Three Types

Projects	Project-Based Learning	Problem-Based Learning (Student-Generated Examples)
Create a commercial about a book you have read. Build a model of the life cycle of a butterfly. Create a 3-D map of one of the countries in the Middle East.	Select an insect mascot for your school. Research the insect and create a realistic mascot. Craft a multimedia presentation to present your creation. Choose an issue in history, such as the Civil Rights Movement or the Equal Rights Movement. In groups, create and perform an original composition. Depending on the age of your students, they might draw a cartoon strip, write a song, or create a video. Use everyday items to create a new invention to present to a group of venture capitalists.	After reading *The Moon Book* by Gail Gibbons, students in an elementary classroom asked, "How long would it take to go to the moon?" In groups, they decided on a method of transportation, such as a rocket or on a light beam, researched the time it would take to make the trip, created a list of needed supplies, and then described their travels. Some wrote a book, others produced a simple video, but all combined creativity with information to demonstrate their learning. In an area secondary school, there was an accident that occurred near the school. Students wanted to prevent future accidents, so they worked in groups to develop a safety plan for drivers. In addition to creating safety information, such as brochures and a short video, groups also worked together to petition for a stoplight at the intersection to make the area safer.

There are several ways you can decide whether to do projects, project-based learning, or problem-based learning; you can provide rigor through all three. One consideration is your time. Projects require more time, specifically in the planning stages, but because you control all aspects of the product, it requires less time overall. When you are planning for project-based learning, you will need time to develop the project, but you also need to plan for additional support. With problem-based learning, there is less time preparing the assignment, since all you need to provide are general guidelines. However, you typically spend more time facilitating the tasks, and because of the open-ended nature of the tasks, it may take more time to assess students' work. You may choose which to use based on when you are able to invest extra time.

Differentiating Projects, Project-Based Learning, and Problem-Based Learning Using Learning Portraits

Although you may differentiate the tasks themselves in projects, project based learning, or problem-based learning, one of the easiest ways to differentiate is to vary which of the three you use with students. For example, your advanced students who are self-motivated are more likely to be successful with problem-based learning, while students who struggle may be more comfortable with the teacher-directed approach of project-based learning. I generally do not recommend traditional projects, as they tend to focus everyone on the amount of time to complete and how creative the products are. They are rarely rigorous, and there is limited teacher support, which means struggling students are less likely to be successful.

Demonstration of Learning Through Genius Hour

Genius Hour is an excellent way to differentiate instruction for students. Genius Hour is inspired by Google's efforts with their employees: 20% of employees' time is motivated by passion and curiosity. They found that their employees were happier, more creative, and more productive. Educators have adapted this for use in a classroom, shifting to the concept of providing students one hour to work on their passions. When we apply this with students, we allow them freedom to design their own learning and explore their own interests, which increases an intrinsic sense of purpose. Many schools are now implementing Genius Hour, which occurs for a minimum of one hour per week. Key principles of Genius Hours are that students take charge of their own learning, including the design of the task, use of inquiry to navigate learning, and the creation of a finished product to demonstrate a deep understanding of their topics.

However, there are some common mistakes that can derail a successful Genius Hour experience for your students.

Common Mistakes

Allowing total choice without providing guidance and support (some structure is needed, particularly as they work on their projects).

Assuming you aren't teaching during Genius Hour (you are teaching in a different way, as a facilitator of learning).

Forgetting to leave time for processing and reflection (critical to success, this also includes feedback from others and you).

Not providing the opportunity to practice the final presentation.

Differentiating Genius Hour Based on Learning Portraits

Inherent in the philosophy of a Genius Hour is the notion that students' topics are driven by things they value. Although you want to give students the widest latitude possible to choose their topics, you may need to provide some guidance, especially for students who are less ready for independent work. I found with my students that it was helpful to provide a list of possible topics they can choose from if they don't have a focus.

Possible Topics for Genius Hour

Ideas for Elementary Students	Ideas for Middle/High School Students
Black Holes Skateboarding Robots How to Take Care of a Dog How to Make Jewelry Saving Water to Help in a Drought How to Improve Smartphones Ways to Make a New Student Feel Welcome How to Choose the Best Pet How to Create a Fun Family Activity	** Some elementary topics are also appropriate for middle/high school Create Website on How to Create a Website How Smartphones Work How to Make a Building Handicap Accessible How Can We Prevent Alzheimer's? How Does Cancer Spread? How Do Butterflies Get Their Colors? How Can You Jump Higher in Basketball?

You will likely need to provide structure and support for Genius Hour. The amount and type of scaffolding will depend on the readiness levels of your students. Once students have chosen a topic, they give an "Elevator Pitch," which is a 3-minute talk proposing the idea. They can present this to other students or to you. They can use feedback from the teacher and students to adjust their proposal. Some students will be able to complete this with no additional guidelines. Others may need a graphic organizer to help them plan; for some, you may need to provide small group coaching.

Guiding Questions for Genius Hour Feedback

What is the overall question you are answering?

What have you done/where are you in the process?

What has changed since you started/since we last talked?

What help do you need from me?

Is there anything else I should know?

The process of investigation is similar, with some students navigating their own learning and others needing some level of guidance and support from you, whether in the form of recommended resources, structured study guides, or small group instruction.

For the final product, all students need the opportunity to practice their presentations. The presentation of the end product also requires varying levels of support based on students' readiness. Interestingly, you may have students who are quite advanced in designing and investigating a topic, but who struggle with the final product. Remember that students' readiness or skill levels can change at different stages. That's why formative assessment is critical.

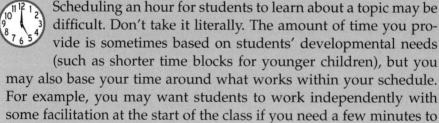

Time Management Tip

Scheduling an hour for students to learn about a topic may be difficult. Don't take it literally. The amount of time you provide is sometimes based on students' developmental needs (such as shorter time blocks for younger children), but you may also base your time around what works within your schedule. For example, you may want students to work independently with some facilitation at the start of the class if you need a few minutes to get organized or touch base with absent students. Or you may want to do Genius Hour at the end of class so that, while facilitating group work, you can also assess their learning of the content from class. It also may be easier to plan for Genius Hour to occur in larger chunks, rather than trying to schedule around other content.

Demonstration of Learning Through Virtual Field Trips

Another effective way to enhance your instruction through technology is to conduct virtual field trips. In today's budget-conscious schools, this is particularly helpful. Imagine the activities you can integrate into the classroom with a virtual tour of the Smithsonian. In the sample below by Abbigail Armstrong, a visit to the Louvre was linked to a study of Egyptian history in grade 6. With adaptations of the assignments, they could easily be used in a high school art class.

The Louvre Visit

Today we are going to take an exciting trip to Paris, France! Your ticket is www.louvre.fr/en and your vehicle is your computer, tablet, or phone. Please read the instructions carefully so your trip is not wasted. I want you to have fun and learn something new in the process. We will have a round-table discussion on our magnificent trip Friday. Have fun, and I can't wait to hear about your adventure!

1. As your tour guide, I suggest you learn some information about the Louvre Museum before you begin your tour. Start at the *Collection and Louvre Palace* link. Read the information about the history of The Louvre. You are in Paris and you call home to talk to someone you love. Tell them about the Louvre's history in 3–5 sentences. Include why the museum was established and how it has been important to France.

2. Now you are ready to take your tour. Using the same link, go to *Online Tours*. Choose the following tour: *Egyptian Antiquities*. Walk around on the floor to several areas. Spend 10 minutes learning how to navigate through the museum floor. Go to the help menu for ways to better navigate the tour.

3. Choose one sculpture from your tour. Analyze how it reflects the culture of Egypt.

---

4. Interpret the artwork. Communicate the artist's statement. Describe what you think the artist is trying to say through the work of art. Expound on the feeling conveyed by the artwork. Describe what the artwork means to you, and why. Explain what you feel is the artist's intended purpose for creating that particular work of art. Examine why the artist made the choices in technique, materials, and subject matter and how they relate to the intended purpose. Your narrative should be approximately one page.

**Note—for more suggestions, visit www.wikihow.com/Critique-Artwork (the suggestions in number 4 are an excerpt from this site).

Ideas for Other Content Areas

Math: Students can plan the trip to the Louvre, look up the flight, and calculate the cost. Social Studies: Plan what to take and how to pack. Discuss how to prepare to visit the country, learn about Paris, and the French government. Also discuss the history of Egypt and the symbolism of the historical time period. Language Arts: How did the authors and poets of Egypt impact the culture? Also teach about critiques and writing the analysis.

It's important to remember that the field trip itself should not be the end result. The goal is increased learning related to your objectives. In the box are several ideas for field trips; however, use your favorite search engine to find a tour that meets your instructional needs.

Sources for Virtual Field Trips

Moon in Google Earth
www.google.com/earth/explore/showcase/moon.html

Smithsonian National Museum of Natural History
http://naturalhistory.si.edu/VT3/#

Liberty Bell
www.nformationdesign.com/portfolio/portfolio07.php

Pyramids at Giza
www.nationalgeographic.com/travel/egypt/pyramids-at-giza/

Great Wall of China
www.airpano.com/360Degree-VirtualTour.php?3D=china-great-wall

Pi Day
www.discoveryeducation.com/PiDay/

International Dot Day (based on the picture book *The Dot*)
www.discoveryeducation.com/Events/monthly-themes/dot-day-2016.cfm

A Celebration of Shakespeare
www.discoveryeducation.co.uk/video/item922104

Farms (various types)
www.farmfood360.ca/?utm_source=domain&utm_campaign=
www.virtualfarmtours.ca&utm_medium=redirect

Differentiating Virtual Field Trips Based on Learning Portraits

The easiest way to differentiate field trips is to allow students to choose the site to explore, based on their interests, overlapping their readiness needs. Advanced students can explore the Internet to find an appropriate field trip and design specific tasks that fit into categories provided by the teacher. Some students might choose a topic and then ask the teacher to assist them in finding an appropriate website. The teacher also provides open-ended questions and tasks for exploration. Finally, struggling students might be allowed to choose from a list of virtual fieldtrips chosen by the teacher (based on students' learning portraits). A guided exploration of the site is provided.

Time Management Tip
It's always helpful to find sites for virtual field trips that other teachers recommend. Ask other teachers in your school or district, but also use social media to get recommendations. Twitter, Facebook, and bulletin boards on teacher sites are great places to ask for other teachers' ideas.

Demonstration of Learning Through Choice

Providing students with structured choices of products is a great way to shift ownership of learning to them. Many teachers use menus, which allow for some required tasks, and others that students may choose.

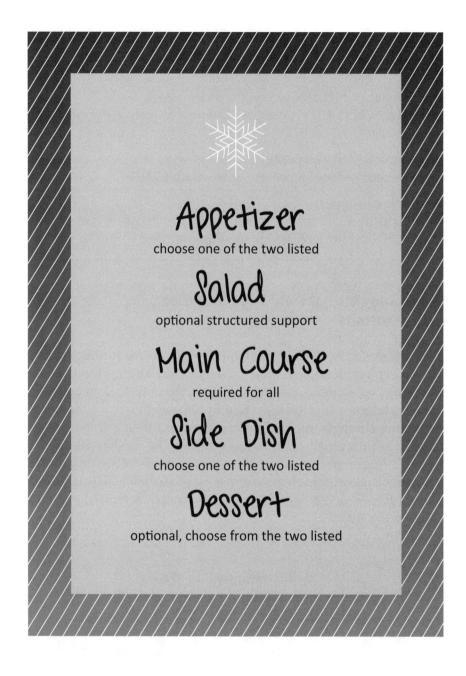

Another alternative is choice boards, or tic-tac-toes. At the end of a unit, rather than assigning the same project for all students, give them a tic-tac-toe board with nine possible assignments. Students choose three in order to create tic-tac-toe. You can structure the assignments so that some are more rigorous than others, but be sure that each one has some rigor built in.

Create a T-chart to share how structures such as carbohydrates, lipids, proteins, DNA, and RNA are related to their functions in plants and animals. **Table:** | Structure	Related to Animal Cell Function	Related to Plant Cell Function
DNA		
RNA		| Justify your responses with at least two pieces of evidence.	The *Mesodinium chamaeleon* is a newly discovered single-celled organism, which is a unique mixture of animal and plant. After reading the article (*https://scitechdaily.com/mesodinium-chamaeleon-is-a-unique-life-form-that-is-half-plant-half-animal/*), write a description of the hybrid organism, including its characteristics, life cycle, food, and how animal and plant cells combined to create the organism.	Create a virus with all of the attributes and describe how that virus must use living cells to reproduce. Use your text and at least two other sources to support your description.
	Using that information, design a comic strip or short graphic novel describing what humans can do to protect these organisms from extinction.	
Using at least three sources, research the effects the environment has on plant and animal cells to include effects such as diseases. Create a presentation to share your findings with your classmates.	Write a two-voices poem for animal and plant cell functions. In your reflection, provide support for your statements.	Create a game about plant and animal cells. Write a reflection that explains why the answers to your questions are correct.

(Continued)

(Continued)

List all of the specialized structures within the animal cell, such as DNA or ribosomes, and describe the structure's function. Next, predict what would happen if one of those structures didn't exist. Support your prediction with evidence.	Create a Venn Diagram to compare the differences and similarities of plant and animal cells. Next, create your own entity that has cells. Add the third circle to your Venn diagram and complete it.	Create a RAFT where you choose the Role, Audience, and Format. Your topic will be to explain how plant cells and animal cells meet the same life needs such as produce, transport, and modify proteins.

Time Management Tip

Creating choice boards, or tic-tac-toes, can be challenging in terms of time and creativity (coming up with nine ideas takes energy). Don't use them all the time; you might start with just one or two a year. This is another tool that is easier if you get help from other teachers. You might also ask students for ideas of how they can "show what they know."

Differentiating Choices Based on Learning Portraits

In any of these formats, choices can be designed based on topics students value. For example, in the menu option, the required main course might be a question that allows students to connect the content to a real-life application of interest. Or, for the appetizers, the teacher could provide one option, and allow students to design and answer the second task.

Choices are oftentimes based on readiness. Notice that, in the following social studies example, all four tasks are rigorous while accommodating varying readiness levels.

Tasks Related to Countries in Africa

Tiered by Readiness Level

1. Using a two-circle Venn diagram, choose two countries from the list and describe how they are alike and different. Create a video or brochure convincing someone why one of the countries is a better place to live. Be sure to provide real-life justifications. (You could enlarge this to three countries.)

2. Choose a country. Investigate what the country was like 100 years ago and what it is like now. Identify and research a famous leader in the country from 100 years ago, and describe how he or she would handle a specific issue in the country today, based on his or her experience.

3. Choose an issue that concerns the people of Africa. Create an advocacy campaign to promote the issue and how it is impacting the population, advocate for a particular stance on the issue, and describe how people in Africa and other countries can help address the issue. Write a reflection that justifies your points.

4. Design a new country that will be part of Africa. Although you cannot change the physical environment or climate from the geographical area of Africa you choose, you may design all other aspects of the country to create one that incorporates the most positive elements from other countries in Africa. Design your own way to present information about your country, which includes an explanation of why you chose particular elements from other countries, and how the combination of elements makes your country a model for others.

A Final Note

Differentiating how students demonstrate understanding of their learning is the ultimate outcome of differentiated instruction. At this point, students "show what they know," and it is imperative that their understanding be at higher levels. One of the most common myths related to differentiation is that teachers should differentiate products by making them "harder" or "easier." While you want to vary in terms of depth and complexity, increasing the number of tasks for advanced learners and adjusting some tasks to measure memorization and recall is not appropriate. As you adjust your options for demonstrating learning based on format and learning portraits, keep in mind that any option should challenge students.

 Points to Ponder

The most important thing I learned was . . .
I was surprised about . . .
I want to learn more about . . .
I'd like to try . . .

6

Managing the Rigorous, Differentiated Classroom

Building a Culture That Supports Rigor and Differentiation

Let's begin our discussion of culture by revising the shared beliefs about rigor and differentiation from Chapter 1.

Revised Shared Beliefs

Shared Beliefs About Rigor and Differentiation	Impact on Classroom Culture
• Every student deserves an equitable opportunity to learn at rigorous levels, which includes providing appropriate support.	• Teacher models that every student is valuable. • Teacher creates an environment in which everyone doing exactly the same thing (equal) is different from making sure each student receives whatever they need to be successful (equitable). • Teacher creates an environment in which all students not only are expected to succeed, but they know they will be able to succeed, perhaps with help. • Scheduling provides time for advanced students to work at higher levels, whether on their own or with teacher support.

(Continued)

(Continued)

Shared Beliefs About Rigor and Differentiation	Impact on Classroom Culture
	• Scheduling provides time for the teacher to work with struggling students. • Scheduling provides this support within the classroom, rather than requiring students to attend outside of class. • Scheduling, especially for group work, is flexible, and therefore, does not label students as being "stuck in the dumb group." • Spacing is also used appropriately, so that, while students can receive appropriate support, there is not a feeling of isolation. • Appropriate resources are used so that all students can be successful at rigorous levels.
• Students can learn essential, rigorous, complex concepts when teachers meet students where they are and help them move forward.	• Although the teacher provides appropriate support through scheduling, resources, and groupings, those aspects ensure that students ultimately master rigorous content.
• Students are individuals who have different needs, strengths, and weaknesses.	• Teacher celebrates the uniqueness of each student, and creates opportunities for students to appreciate each other. • Teacher understands each individual student (through learning profiles, observations, and regular contact) and creates an environment that not only allows for those differences, but addresses them to help each student learn at high levels. • Teacher provides scheduling, resources, and grouping to address individual needs.

Shared Beliefs About Rigor and Differentiation	Impact on Classroom Culture
• We should create a classroom environment and instruction that addresses all aspects of students' needs.	• Scheduling is flexible and varied groupings to meet all students' needs are a normal part of the classroom. • A variety of resources at a range of levels are provided throughout the classroom so that all students' needs are met, whether they are struggling or advanced.

Notice that there are common threads that reflect our beliefs, especially related to scheduling, space, resources, and groupings. Just for general consideration, don't forget about student motivation, student ownership of learning, and encouraging student independence.

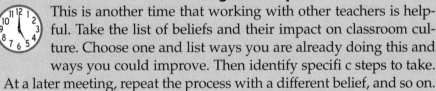

Time Management Tip

This is another time that working with other teachers is helpful. Take the list of beliefs and their impact on classroom culture. Choose one and list ways you are already doing this and ways you could improve. Then identify specifi c steps to take. At a later meeting, repeat the process with a different belief, and so on. Focusing on one at a time will lead to lasting change.

Organizational Elements

While managing the rigorous, differentiated classroom, we need to consider several organizational elements.

Organizational Elements

Scheduling

Space

Resources

Routines

Grouping Strategies

Working With Absentee Students

Scheduling

There are a variety of ways to build a schedule in a differentiated class-room. The rule of thumb should be *do what works and is best for students*. There will be days you can keep your whole group together, mixing in partner work or times for students to work individually. More often than not, you will need to provide tiering activities, with students moving in and out of groups, providing group activities based on interest (which may include cultural interests), or providing work in learning centers. It's also important to consider planning from a long-term perspective rather than individual lessons.

Sample Schedule for Middle or High School Classroom

(Sample Only; May Take Multiple Days)		
Whole Group: Introduction to Lesson		
Individual/Partner Activity: Completion of Anticipation Guide as a warm-up and activation of prior knowledge (see sample instructions below)		
Whole Group: Initial Instruction, through discussion, lecture, discovery-based lesson, video clips, etc.		
Whole Group: Application Activity		
Tiered Activities by Readiness		
Tier One	Tier Two	Tier Three
Teacher working with small group providing support and instruction on specific skills to ensure students are working at a rigorous level.	Students working with partners on a parallel activity that applies the content in a new way.	Students working independently on an extension activity.

Whole Class and Small Groups: Discussion, review, and additional tiering as needed		
Small Groups by Interests		
Interest One	Interest Two	Interest Three
Students work in interest-based groups, with teacher support and facilitation as needed. Specific roles and responsibilities are either assigned or provided by the teacher so each student will participate.	Students work in interest-based groups, with teacher support and facilitation as needed. Specific roles and responsibilities are either assigned or provided by the teacher so each student will participate.	Students work in interest-based groups, with teacher support and facilitation as needed. Specific roles and responsibilities are either assigned or provided by the teacher so each student will participate.
Whole Group: Presentation of Interest-Based Group Projects		

Sample Schedule for Elementary Thematic Reading and Writing Lesson

(Sample Occurs Over Multiple Days)			
Whole Group: Circle activity: Introduction of lesson and activation of background knowledge			
Whole Group: Circle activity: Read-Aloud and classroom discussion			
Tiered Activities by Readiness			
Teacher works with students who need guided support as they read related text in small group. The small group answers application questions related to the text.	Students work with partners to read a related text, using a Guide-O-Rama (see Chapter 3), and complete application questions related to the text.	Students work independently or with a partner to read a related text at a higher level and complete application questions related to the text.	
Whole Group: Discussion of related texts and connections among all texts; introduction to learning centers and culminating activity			
Rotation Through Learning Centers to Prepare for Culminating Assignment (All Students Rotate Through All Stations)			
LC One: Reading	LC Two: Writing	LC Three: Viewing and Listening	LC Four: Connections to Other Subject Areas and Real World Based on Interests

Students read informational article connected to the topic of earlier texts. They can work independently, with a partner, or with the small group to read the text; graphic organizers, recording of text, and other support materials are provided if needed so that students can compare the informational text to the earlier texts.	Students write or draw a comic strip of a new ending to one of the texts read in a small group or in the tiered lesson. The new ending must show a clear connection to events and characters in the original text, as well as including a real-life example.	Students watch a short video; either an interview with the author of the initial text, a video about the general topic of the text (such as alligators), or another related text. They complete a short reflection on what they learned.	Students work independently, with a partner, or in the small group to go back through the original text and identify and write 2–3 sentences connecting the text to a real-life situation or other text (written text, Internet material, movie, or TV show), based on their interests. For students who need additional help, guidance can be provided, such as directing students to sources related to a real-life connection of interest.

Whole Group: Discussion of learning center activities and introduction of culminating writing activity: write a new story related to their life that connects elements from all information and activities. Students read their stories to the class and explain how their story is based on the other texts (justification). Multiple activities occur throughout the writing and presentation process, including tiered mini-lessons, peer reviews (with questioning guides if needed), and individual writing conferences.

Space

A differentiated classroom requires a different consideration of space. The traditional setup of rows, or even some types of table arrangements, do not facilitate flexible groupings. There is not a perfect way to design your classroom because you may have a smaller or larger room, you may have a small alcove just outside your room, or you may have a door that opens to a small grassy area. It also makes a difference whether you have additional chairs or other seating and whether you have room for resources. Typically, although not always, elementary school classrooms have more space than high school ones, and middle school rooms fall somewhere in between.

Ideally, you would have space for whole class instruction with designated areas that have appropriate seating for small groups and independent workstations. One suggested floor plan is below.

If there is no extra space other than the standard desks or tables where students sit for whole-group instruction, then you will simply have to rearrange chairs as needed.

In a sixth grade classroom I visited, teachers Angie Krakeel and Kelly Zorn had different zones in the room. Some of the zones were sections of the classroom, the success zone was a section of the wall, and some, such as the quiet zone, could be at the student's original seat. Throughout the day, students in small groups moved from the reading zone to the technology zone, and so on.

Possible Zones for an Elementary Classroom

Reading

Writing

Words and Vocabulary

Technology

Success Zone (posting of student work)

Quiet Zone (for independent work)

MakerSpace

Drama/Music/Art

Science

Interest (contains items students choose based on their interests)

Time Management Tip

Space is tricky. You are bound by your four walls and the furniture you have (unless your administrator will provide funding for additional space). At the beginning of the year, develop a plan for how you will use your space. Revisit it a few weeks later and adapt it to be more effective. Then, as long as it is working, leave it alone.

Resources

There are two considerations for resources in a rigorous, differentiated classroom. With a focus on providing appropriate materials for all students based, in part, on their learning profiles, you'll want to have a wide range of text-based and technology-based resources.

Selection of Internet-Based Resources

Source	Information
www.watchknowlearn. org/About.aspx	Over 50,000 videos appropriate for students in all content areas and all grade levels.
www.khanacademy.org	Khan Academy is one of the best-known and widely used sites for videos, especially for the math classroom. Although the math lessons are for elementary, middle, and high school students, there are other subject lessons for middle and high school.

(Continued)

(Continued)

Source	Information
www.edudemic.com/best-video-sites-for-teachers/	Edudemic's article provides their best 100 recommendations for video sites.
www.pbslearningmedia.org	PBS's site provides a variety of engaging instructional videos, web pages, audio files, and other support for all subject areas and grade levels.
https://ed.ted.com/lessons?category=visual-arts	TedEd lessons are also for all grade ranges and most subject areas.

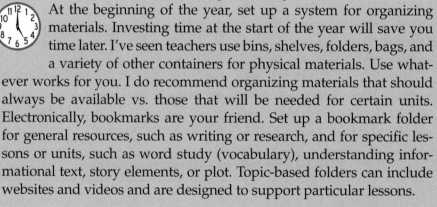

Time Management Tip

At the beginning of the year, set up a system for organizing materials. Investing time at the start of the year will save you time later. I've seen teachers use bins, shelves, folders, bags, and a variety of other containers for physical materials. Use whatever works for you. I do recommend organizing materials that should always be available vs. those that will be needed for certain units. Electronically, bookmarks are your friend. Set up a bookmark folder for general resources, such as writing or research, and for specific lessons or units, such as word study (vocabulary), understanding informational text, story elements, or plot. Topic-based folders can include websites and videos and are designed to support particular lessons.

A second challenge with resources is to provide materials that lead students to rigorous work. For example, in a science class, students may need access to experiments at different readiness levels that all lead students to the same complex conclusions and recommendations. In a social studies classroom focusing on current events, students in interest-based groups should be able to find materials on their subject at a variety of reading levels to help them learn the essential concepts. Similarly, if students are in tiered groups based on readiness, they should have access to text materials, such as books and articles, that are written at different levels.

For example, if I am teaching a lesson on biomes, but a group of my students cannot read the article, I would use an easier article on the same topic with students. However, in order to ensure rigor, I then guide students through the original article. They are more likely to succeed because, by reading the easier article, they have built background knowledge and vocabulary. My advanced students are reading the original article, then an advanced article to enhance their understanding. While this strategy, called layering meaning, is particularly effective, it requires specialized resources. Print materials for different levels are available for purchase, but there are free options available online.

Sources for Leveled Text

In early 2018, unless noted, these are free, but sites may add premium items or add a fee at a later time.

- Newsela (https://newsela.com) provides several different levels of the same news article; students can read for free; a small fee allows teachers to monitor progress. They also provide some texts in Spanish.
- News in Levels (www.newsinlevels.com) and For the Teachers (www.fortheteachers.org/reading_skills/) also provide varying levels of an article or text. For the Teachers has science, health, and other topics, but information is language arts oriented.
- Books That Grow (www.booksthatgrow.com) has a library of texts that have each been edited to be made accessible to different reading levels. There is a fee.
- TweenTribune (http://tweentribune.com) is produced by the Smithsonian. It also provides an article at different levels, but adds a quiz (moderately high level questions) and allows teachers to create virtual classrooms to monitor progress and moderate comments.
- Readworks (www.readworks.org) provides a wide variety of support, including levels of text, audio support for comprehension questions, and highlighting and annotation options.
- Text Compactor (www.textcompactor.com) lets you paste text into it and then automatically summarizes it (with a customized setting you control).
- Rewordify (http://rewordify.com) allows a teacher or student to paste text into the screen, and it will identify challenging words and replace them with simpler ones or with explanations.

Thanks to Larry Ferlazzo for these sources.

Routines

When students are learning, there are clear routines that provide a sense of stability and predictability in the midst of activity. Routines are essential in a differentiated classroom, as students will be transitioning to different activities. It is a balancing act, providing enough variety to meet students' needs while adding enough structure and routine for them to feel a sense of control and predictability. Despite any protests to the contrary, students generally thrive when there is a clear system in place they can depend on and predict.

Although Connie Forrester describes the importance of routines for her kindergarten students, routines are essential for students at all grade levels.

> If there is one element that is crucial to the success of a teacher, then it is structures and schedules. Young children thrive on schedules and find security in knowing the routine. Routines and structures are equally as important as schedules, because without solid routines the schedule would not be as effective. At the beginning of each year, I would carefully walk the children through the day and tell my expectations of each segment. By having clear expectations, it also allowed the children to become risk takers and have ownership in the classroom.

Time Management Tip

Invest time during the first few weeks of school teaching routines. Although it takes away some of your instructional time, you will actually regain that time by cutting down on all the classroom interruptions that happen when students don't understand the routines. You'll be able to simply refer to the routines and reinforce them.

Types of Routines

Types of Routines

Asking and Answering Questions

Activities for Students Who Finish Work Early

Routines for Absent Students

Asking and Answering Questions

Asking questions for students to answer is a standard classroom activity. However, there are two routines we need to address: ensuring participation of all students and supporting students who struggle to answer questions.

Ensuring Participation of All Students

In a classroom discussion, it's typical to see a few students who dominate the conversation. Sometimes, they blurt out the answer before they are called on. There are also times that we unintentionally ignore certain students. Finally, some students are not sure of their answer, so they choose not to respond, even if we call on them. Therefore, we need to have routines that address these issues.

Routines for Successful Student Responses

- Include a 15-second "Think About It" time before anyone can answer.
- Allow students to work with a partner or in small groups to determine the answer prior to sharing out loud, in order to help them be successful.
- Use responses in the whole-group setting that allow for each student to participate, such as duo-response cards, individual whiteboards, thumbs up or down, or technology options.
- Use individual notes or post-its for students to provide anonymous responses that you can use, particularly for review.
- Give each student 2 or 3 tokens. Each time they respond, they must give up a token. (Note: I don't recommend this except with students who are totally dominating the class).
- Use a checklist and mark each time you call on a student.
- Pull popsicle sticks with students' names.
- Distribute playing cards to students and call on a card.
- Use a spinner system or roll a die to determine which small group to respond.

Keep in mind that your goal is for equitable (not necessarily equal) participation. And let me add a caveat. There will be times that you need to determine which student to call on based on your teacher judgment. This is absolutely valid. Incorporating some of the routines we have discussed ensures that we don't ignore students, even if it is subconscious.

Time Management Tip

Because questioning is such a critical part of classroom instruction, pay particular attention as to which of these strategies addresses the biggest challenge related to questioning. For example, if a few students are dominating, either use tokens or random questioning. Tackle your biggest challenge first.

Providing Guidance for Student Success

When I was a teacher, one of my challenges was guiding the conversation. During a group discussion, if a student answered correctly, I knew to say, "That's exactly on point." Or "That's a great response that hits the nail on the head." But when a student was incorrect or only partially answered the question, I was stuck. What do you say then? On page 163 you will find a feedback chart that describes how to handle each of those situations. When you are giving students an opportunity to look up information or work with a partner, this is another occasion for differentiation. Some students will only need the extra chance or time to provide an answer; others will need you to guide them, perhaps in terms of narrowing down where students should look for the information.

You will also need to consider creating a method that students can use when they have a question or need help, but they don't want to ask it in front of their classmates. Some teachers use red cups, which students can place on their desks or on top of their computers if they need help. Other less obtrusive options include placing a bright post-it note on the corner of their desk or table, waiting until the teacher is near and signaling for their attention, and allowing students to write a question or post a sticky note anonymously on a white board near the pencil sharpener or in another easy-to-reach location.

Time Management Tip

When determining a strategy students can use to ask for help, choose one that is unobtrusive. If you aren't sure what will work, ask students to help you identify what will.

Grouping Strategies

Flexible groupings are foundational to a differentiated classroom. There are four main types of sizing for groups.

Group Sizes

Type of Group	Advantages	Disadvantages
Whole Group	Same directions for all Teacher-directed Time savings All students hear everyone else's responses	Difficult to manage Hard to differentiate Easy for students to get off-task Less individual participation
Small Group	Combines views and ideas Focuses on cooperation Teaches tolerance Fosters active student learning	Off-task socializing Difficult to assess individual work Unequal sharing of responsibilities May create power struggles or domination of group by one or two students
Partners	Opportunities for engagement Fosters student-focused learning Builds trust	Shared ownership of product Difficult to assess individual work Off-task socializing May not carry equal workload
Alone	Individual accountability Work at own pace and level of need Makes individual choices	No opportunity to learn from others May practice incorrectly No interdependence

Adapted from: Chapman, C., & King, R. (2005). *Differentiated assessment strategies: One tool doesn't fit all.* Thousand Oaks, CA: Corwin Press.

Time Management Tip

When I was teaching, many of my students were not comfortable working in groups. They also had issues getting along. I didn't jump into groups of five or six students unless it was a group I was facilitating based on readiness. I started with partners and groups of three. It made classroom management easier.

There are also different types of groups in terms of who is chosen for each group.

Types of Grouping

Knowledge-Based Groups

Interest Groups

Readiness Groups

Random Groups

Pairs

Other Groups Based on Learning Portraits

Roles for Group Members

A critical step is structuring your group activity so that each student has a specific way to participate. In tiered groupings, or when the teacher is facilitating a group, you may not need to assign roles, but when students are working in interest-based groups, makerspaces, or other choice-based groups, you will need to either assign roles or allow students to choose or create a role. The roles may change depending on your assignment. For example, if students are working on a lab experiment, you will need a safety monitor and a materials manager. However, if your project is developing a web page, you might prefer a webmaster and a layout editor.

Sample Roles and Responsibilities

Facilitator—Leader of the group; facilitates action

Recorder—Records comments and/or work

Reporter—Reports work to the entire group

Materials Manager—Collects and distributes materials

Timekeeper—Keeps the group working within time limits

Technology Manager—Coordinates technology use

Encourager—Encourages others

Summarizer—Summarizes work and may report to the class

Fact Checker—Checks work from group; researches facts

Reflector—Reflects on comments from group; asks probing questions

Designer—Designs the project

Creator—Creates or builds the design

I encourage you to rotate the roles within the team for different assignments so that one or two students do not dominate the group activities. You should also take time to teach students about their roles and responsibilities.

Time Management Tip

Don't recreate the wheel. There are many lists of roles on the Internet. Start with those and adapt.

Rules

In addition to your standard classroom rules, you may need a couple of simple rules that are specific to group activities. I found that I needed to discuss my expectations for the noise level of the classroom. For example, I wanted my students to talk to each other. But they needed to talk to their group members, not the entire class. You might come up with a catchy way to describe an appropriate noise level, such as "Bees Buzz." Bees buzz when they are being productive (making honey), but they don't shout. I was in another classroom in which the teacher talked about using your "12-inch voice." Her students knew that meant that people within a foot (within the group) should be able hear you, but not those outside the group (more than a foot away).

I also used a rule called "ask three before me." This one works when your students are in groups of four. It simply means that a student should ask his or her group members for help before asking the teacher. This encourages students to look to each other for support instead of always looking to the teacher first. It's up to you to decide what rules you need in your classroom. Be sure that your students understand your expectations, and monitor the groups continuously to ensure that all students have an opportunity to participate.

Finally, you may want to use talking chips, a strategy in which you give each student three chips or tokens. Each time a student speaks, he or she must turn in his or her chip (in a bag in the center of the group). When a student is out of chips, he or she is not allowed to talk until all other students have turned in their chips.

Earlier, Angie Krakeel and Kelly Zorn shared how they set up their classrooms with zones. They also provided a set of procedures they use with their students to facilitate work in those zones.

Policies and Procedures for Zones

- When we are in zones, do not interrupt Mrs. Zorn or Ms. Krakeel.
- If you have questions:
    - First, try to find the answer on your own. Read!
    - Second, find help from others in your zone.
    - Third, write the question or problem down to be addressed by us during a transition time.
- Transitions should happen quickly. When time is up, time is up. You will have at least one other opportunity to complete the task that you are working on. Clean up your area and quietly move to your next zone.

Transitions

Because your students will be moving into a variety of groupings, you will want to have routines for smooth transitions. First, you need to determine a set of routines, teach them to students, and then regularly reinforce them.

Sample Transitional Routines

Once you hear the signal, move to your assignment space. When you hear the second signal, you should be in your space.

Toward the end of the work session, you'll hear a signal that indicates it is time to finish. Two minutes later, you'll hear the signal to move to your next location.

Although moving around the classroom can be noisy, there is an acceptable level of noise. If you see the lights flicker, take it down a notch.

Time Management Tip

Once again, teach the routines for group work when students are first asked to work together. Don't wait until problems start. It takes longer to fix a problem than to prevent one.

Addressing Challenges

No matter how well prepared you are or how effectively you teach ways students can work in groups, you will still face some challenges. There are standard strategies you can use to respond to these issues.

Strategies for Dealing With Challenges

When a Student . . .	*You Can . . .*
Doesn't like working in groups	Reinforce the positive aspects of working in groups Praise him or her for successes in group work Provide some opportunities for student to work alone but stress the importance of group work
Has a personality clash with another group member	Teach strategies for effective group work Provide some opportunities for student to work alone, but stress the importance of group work Discuss the issue with both students, and facilitate problem-solving strategies Monitor, and if needed, move student to a different group
Doesn't participate in or do his or her part with the group	Teach strategies for effective group work Assign roles and responsibilities to group members Incorporate individual and group accountability
Is bored and doesn't want to participate because he or she is gifted or advanced	Provide rigorous work as an authentic part of the group activity for all students, but tailor a portion of the work at a higher level so that gifted and advanced students are appropriately challenged without being punished by simply completing more work or the work of others

Activities for Students Who Finish Work Early

When I was a student teacher, one of my biggest challenges was determining what to do with students when they finished their work early. My supervising teacher had a simple solution. She asked me to create a file folder for each student, and she provided worksheets I copied and put in each folder. Anytime a student finished their work, they were required to complete as many worksheets as needed to fill the time. Students felt as though they were being punished for mastering work early. This demonstrates one of the myths of rigor: that rigor equals more work.

Lorenzo, a seventh grader, was in a classroom where, if he finished work early, he could work on his homework or do anything he wanted, as long as he was quiet. That's also not a positive alternative.

A better alternative is to have a set of acceptable routines students can follow when they complete their work. I visited a kindergarten classroom where the teacher and the students worked together to create a tic-tac-toe that identified nine differentiated activities for early work completion. Not only did this create a smooth solution to classroom management, students felt ownership in the activities because they helped create them.

One of the common challenges in managing any classroom, especially one that is differentiated, is how to handle students who are absent. Nothing replaces the student actually attending class, but there are alternatives.

Many teachers use some format so that when students return after an absence, they are able to pick up copies of missed work.

Tips for Providing Assignments for Absent Students

Have a common location for papers.

Use a binder with color-coded work for middle and high school classes.

Have a set of student mailboxes for elementary students; place work in the mailbox for the student (mailbox can also be used for other purposes).

Put an empty folder on an absent student's desk and fill it as you hand out work.

Have a separate folder available for students who will be going on a trip or vacation so they may get their work in advance.

If another student is a neighbor of the absent student, and is willing, ask him or her to deliver materials.

Many teachers take advantage of technology to facilitate students' make-up work. If you have a web page, blog, or online portal, post your assignments and accompanying material on the page. I think this works as a routine so that other students have access, particularly if they misplace a handout. If you have students or parents/families who have regular access to email, it's easy to email material so students have access before they return to class. If appropriate to your content, provide a link to a YouTube video or a presentation that you created that presents the material.

Another way to provide support for the absent student is to use other students to share what they learned with the student when he or she returns to class. Of course, you are likely to do a review of material with all students, but friends can provide additional information. I also like to have students complete exit slips with what they learned and then provide relevant slips to the absent student. After students have offered support, you can then provide individualized help.

You'll also want to consider rigor and differentiation when working with absentee students. It may not be necessary for them to complete every assignment they missed, as long as they can demonstrate understanding of the material at a rigorous level. I've worked with teachers who compact the assignments, provide alternative assignments, or even waive assignments. With the flexible scheduling used in a differentiated classroom, consider providing extra time during class for students to catch up on work. I met an art teacher who built in a "finish up" day just before a project was due to allow not only for absentee students, but for others who needed a bit more time.

Ways for Students to Catch Up on Instruction

Watch a video of the teacher's presentation

Watch a YouTube video that presents similar content

Provide written materials to support learning

Ask all students to write what they learned and share with student

When the student returns to class, pair him or her with another student for review

Place student in a tiered group as needed

Provide one on one time with student

Finally, you will want to have a system or routine for students to show you they understand the missed content, whether that is verbally or through turning in assignments. First, it's important to set a deadline that is appropriate to complete or master the material. I found that insisting on completion of work one day after a student's return was not feasible, especially if they needed to complete more than one assignment in an elementary classroom, or if they missed work in multiple classes in middle and high schools. There is not an exact formula to use; you'll need to use your judgment to determine a time that meets your expectations and allows for the student's needs. If you want to discuss the material with a student to determine what they have learned, schedule a short amount of time as a part of your flexible grouping for that to occur. I observed one teacher who, rather than asking the student to simply tell him what she learned, provided an opportunity to "reteach" the material to a small group. Then, he asked follow-up questions. If you have written work for students to turn in, create a system and routine, perhaps with a bright folder on your desk.

Time Management Tip

Ask other teachers what works for them. Create a system that is practical and not too complicated. It sounds nice to have a cute crate with colorful folders that have pictures on them. Keep it simple. At middle and high school, something for each class period; at elementary, one per day. Cute is nice, but not necessary. Once you have the system working the way you want it to, then go back and decorate if you like.

A Final Note

Managing and organizing your classroom is critical in a differentiated, rigorous classroom. Planning for appropriate scheduling, use of space, resources, routines, effective group work, and procedures for students who are absent are important factors in effective instruction.

Points to Ponder

The most important thing I learned was . . .
I was surprised about . . .
I want to learn more about . . .
I'd like to try . . .

7

Common Concerns

Although we have discussed the major concepts of differentiation, as well as looking at practical ideas for implementation, I wanted to address the common concerns I hear most often from teachers.

Common Concerns

Time

Teaching Standards

Homework

Grading

Gifted and Advanced Learners

Differentiation, Personalization, and Individualization

Communicating With Parents and Families

Working With Leaders

Time

How can I find the time to create lessons, find resources, and grade assignments or tests for students working at all these different levels?

There is no doubt that this is the number one concern of teachers considering rigorous, differentiated instruction. With everything teachers must juggle to be effective, rigorous differentiation can seem overwhelming. I'm often asked what would be my ideal solution. That's easy. I'd schedule every Friday as a professional day, providing ample time for teachers to work together to plan, assess, learn new ideas, and improve teaching. Unfortunately, that is not reality, and I don't have a magic wand. So, what do we do?

Hopefully you noticed time management tips throughout the chapters in this book. Those are short ideas that can be used on the spot. Here, let's look at some bigger recommendations for addressing the concern. I'm going to give you a two-part answer.

Two-Part Answer

Adjusting to Your Current Situation

Advocating for Change

Adjusting to Your Current Situation

I would encourage you to advocate for what you need on an ongoing basis. However, while you are working to change the situation, there are strategies that will help you accept your current status.

Strategies for Your Current Situation

1. Accept that you will never have as much time or as many resources as you would like.

2. Accept that the quest for perfectionism may be your enemy.

3. Work with other teachers.

4. Create a Personal Learning Network.

5. Work smarter, not harder.

6. Remember that small changes lead to bigger ones.

7. Keep balance in your life.

Strategy 1: Accept that you will never have as much time or as many resources as you would like. I continue to find that, no matter how much I have to do, I always need more time. I told a friend of mine once that I wished I had 48 hours per day. She replied, "If that happened, you would end up with double the work!" I find inspiration from Maya Angelou: *If you don't like something, change it. If you can't change it, change your attitude. Don't complain.*

Strategy 2: Accept that the quest for perfectionism may be your enemy. I have realized that there are times my expectations for myself are too high and are, at times, unrealistic. I've also found that to be true with many teachers. They spend hours on the Internet looking up ideas to create the perfect lesson plan when they could have accomplished just as much if they had stopped much earlier. I'm not recommending you provide sloppy instruction. What I am saying is that most of the time, 80% of excellence is still very, very good. If it takes you double or triple the time to gain that additional 20%, it's probably not worth it because of all the other tasks you didn't accomplish.

Strategy 3: Work with other teachers. Although it takes time to meet with other teachers to plan together, in the long run, it saves time. Let's say that you have an upcoming unit in a history class that includes reading a primary source that is likely to be challenging for some students. You need a support tool for struggling students, and that will be needed multiple times during the year. Working with the two other teachers who also teach the same subject and grade level, you divide the work. You write the interactive study guide that some students will need for this unit. Your neighbor writes one for Unit 3, and the teacher down the hall is going on maternity leave, but volunteers to create one for Unit 6 when she returns. Yes, it takes time for you to write one, but you end up with three when you share, which saves you time in the long run.

Time Management Tip

Don't necessarily schedule different times to work on projects. Accomplish as much as you can during regular meetings. Also, make individual assignments (such as interactive reading guides) and set a deadline for completion.

Strategy 4: Create a Personal Learning Network. Sometimes you and your colleagues will need other ideas. I spoke with a teacher who waited until the last minute to plan lessons, then frantically searched the Internet for ideas. If you have ever done that, you know that you have to filter through a lot of mediocre ideas before you find ones you like. Instead, consider creating your own Personal Learning Network (PLN). It's a way of using the Internet and social media to manage your own learning and to organize the information you receive. PLNs are not new. Often, they are just networks of professional contacts, but with social media it's possible to add experts and colleagues from around the world to your network.

Time Management Tip

Set a timer for how long you will explore Personal Learning Networks. I've found that if I don't, I look up and I've been wandering around for hours!

Strategy 5: Work smarter, not harder. You've probably heard this before, but it is true. Far too often, we spend extra time on our work because we can't find something we need, or we don't remember something we wanted to change this year. It is absolutely critical to stay organized so that we streamline what we do. Find or create an organizational system that will help you manage all your tasks. There are technology-based options, as well as paper ones. I find it particularly helpful to have strategies to document changes I want to make when I teach a lesson next year, collect resources I want to use, and keep up with recurring tasks, such as a weekly email to parents.

When I was a teacher, I addressed the first option by writing notes on my plans. The problem was that I wasn't organized enough to find all my notes when I needed them. Now, to keep up with resources I want to use in the future, I use folders for organization. I keep paper folders, folders in my email, and bookmark folders for my browser, all of which include resources and information I can use. One tip I've learned is that I need to have specific topic names on folders, rather than just a miscellaneous label, which makes it more difficult to find resources.

Examples of Folders

Videos

Sample Lessons

Teaching Tips

Sites for Virtual Field Trips

Blogs

State Standards and Resources Related to Standards

Specific Topics on a Subject (such as force and motion, properties and change, and conservation and transfer) **again, it's better to be specific, even if you have more folders*

In terms of recurring tasks, I currently use a to-do list app that allows me to check a box if it occurs regularly, and it automatically schedules it (for example, on the last day of the month). A friend of mine, Frank Buck, provides practical ideas and resources on organization and time management, especially using technology, on his website: www.frankbuck.org.

Strategy 6: Remember that small changes lead to bigger ones. Far too often, we think that if we are implementing something new, we need to change everything we are doing. If you remember the old fable, the turtle finished before the hare in the race. Start slowly, implementing an idea or two at a time, rather than throwing out everything you are doing and starting over. Begin with two tiers one day each week, and then increase them over time. Regular progress is the goal.

Quotes to Encourage You

Never discourage anyone who continually makes progress, no matter how slow . . . even if that someone is yourself!

Plato

No matter how many mistakes you make or how slow you progress, you are still way ahead of everyone who isn't trying.

Tony Robbins

Far away there in the sunshine are my highest aspirations. I may not reach them, but I can look up and see their beauty, believe in them, and try to follow where they lead.

Louisa May Alcott

I'm a slow walker, but I never walk back.

Abraham Lincoln

Painting is a slow process; it takes time to get there, you learn little by little and always want the next painting to be better than the last. For me, success is about this, seeing the slow progress in my work.

Ali Banisadr

We may encounter many defeats but we must not be defeated.

Maya Angelou

Time Management Tip

Keep a small journal or Word document to log your successes at the end of a day (take just 2 minutes and don't wait until the end of the week; you'll forget items) so you can see your progress.

Strategy 7: Keep balance in your life. As you are creating a rigorous, differentiated classroom, you will likely become overwhelmed, tired, and discouraged at times. If you want to make a difference with your students, don't work so much that you don't have time for yourself and your family. Set a time to leave at the end of the day, and stick to it unless there is an emergency. If you need to take work home at night or on the weekend, set a limit of how long you will work. Do your job effectively, but make time for yourself.

Websites That Provide Tips for Work-Life Balance

- www.weareteachers.com/best-of-teacher-helpline-9-tips-for-balancing-work-and-family/
- www.theguardian.com/teacher-network/teacher-blog/2013/jun/25/teacher-work-life-balance-stress-tips
- www.theeducator.com/blog/teacher-work-life-balance-5-tips-for-how-to-have-a-life/

- https://education.cu-portland.edu/blog/classroom-resources/five-tips-for-teacher-work-life-balance/
- https://pernillesripp.com/2016/01/18/12-ways-i-got-my-life-back-in-balance-as-a-teacher/
- www.teachervision.com/blog/morning-announcements/achieving-work-life-balance
- www.maneuveringthemiddle.com/work-life-balance-teachers/

Advocating for Change

In 2017, I was very excited to write a book, *Advocacy From A to Z*, with my father and Ron Williamson from Eastern Michigan University. Since my dad has always been my inspiration, it was a special experience. I also learned there are many facets to advocacy. It's more than just supporting elected officials through our votes. I have excerpted small portions of the book here to help you consider how you can be an advocate.

Everyone is an advocate, whether you recognize it or not. We advocate for our favorite teams, political candidates, and, of course, we advocate for our schools and the resources and programs vital to the success of our students.

Advocacy is what you do when you are actively supporting a cause, such as expanding the time and resources for teaching in a differentiated classroom. Advocacy is a way to systematically press for change. It is also the foundation of our democracy and a process that allows ordinary people to shape and influence policy at all levels. Identifying priorities, crafting a strategy, taking action, and achieving results are critical steps to finding one's voice, making oneself heard, and shaping one's future.

There are five major reasons to become an advocate.

Reasons to Become an Advocate

1. Decisions will be made whether you are involved or not.
2. You have important grass-roots knowledge that decision-makers need to know.
3. Decisions will impact you whether you are involved or not.
4. Advocacy starts with one, and that one is you.
5. You are an advocate—either active or passive.

Once you decide you are an advocate, you want to be an effective one. There are eight characteristics of an effective advocate.

Characteristics of an Effective Advocate

Always listens and learns

Deliberate focus on long-term goals

Values support from others

Openness to different ways to share message

Commitment to partnering with different and like-minded individuals

Ability to look at and respond to positions and an issue

Tenacity to bounce back from negative responses

Engages the public and stakeholders

Stakeholders

Next, you will need to identify the stakeholders who are impacted by your desire for more time and resources. There are three types of local groups that can impact your activities. First, there are those in elected positions. Next, you have internal stakeholders who are connected with your school. Finally, there are external stakeholders. The following chart identifies the contacts that are essential for you to involve in your local efforts.

Essential Stakeholders

Elected*	Internal	External
Mayor County/Town Manager Town Council County Administrator School Superintendent School Board Members	Teachers Staff Students Administrative Team PTAs/PTOs	Families Community Movers and Shakers Non-Profits Media Business Leaders Senior Citizens Local Colleges Community Colleges

*Note: Depending on your local situation, some of those listed under elected officials may be appointed.

Principles of Effective Communication

Be sure to have a clear and concise message. Although your overall message will stay the same (providing teachers additional time to collaborate to improve instruction and providing additional resources we need to meet the needs of all students), you may customize points for different audiences. There are ten principles of effective communication.

---

10 Principles of Effective Communication

Conciseness and consistency matter

Open with your key point

Match to your agenda

Make it coherent

Understand your audience

Name your objective/desired action

Courtesy rules

Ask questions

Tell a story

Empathy helps

Communicating With Your School Board

Finally, let's look at how those tips can play out in a school setting. Following are strategies to communicate with your school board. Consider how these approaches utilize the information we described earlier in the chapter.

Interacting With Your School Board

◆ Identify a parent, student, or community spokesperson to help deliver your message to the board.

◆ Frame the importance of having the right tools for an effective, rigorous, differentiated classroom in your opening statement. Link it to board goals and how students will be successful once they leave your school.

- Describe your plan in such a way that the board can see the link between your overall school improvement efforts and their goals.

- Share examples of your work to illustrate the impact. It can be very helpful to highlight the effect of greater rigor on one or more students.

- Give recognition to the individuals who have contributed to your success. It is a time for you to be modest and allow others to be recognized.

- Conclude your presentation by aligning your vision with the board's vision for the district.

Time Management Tip

Don't go it alone! Work with teachers from your school, other schools in your district or state, and your leaders. Also access support from professional associations, such as ASCD, NEA, or AFT. Joining others means you don't have to start from scratch.

You may have been expecting me to recommend a program that would manage everything for you, or the perfect lesson planning tool that would automatically create your tiers. The perfect tool doesn't exist; if it did, you would be using it. Continue to advocate to your leaders for additional time and resources, but consider these strategies while you accept what you have.

Teaching Standards

If I am providing differentiated instruction, will I still be able to teach all my standards? I'm worried that if I allow some students to work at a slower pace, we won't finish before standardized testing.

This concern has increased along with the emphasis on standardized testing. When part of my salary is based on my students' test scores, I don't want to do anything that will negatively impact the scores. Unfortunately, we can't guarantee our students will be successful, as much as we might want to. Our job is to ensure that we are teaching the standards that standardized tests are based on in a rigorous, engaging way, providing the needed support so that all students master the content. We also need to use some assessments that mimic the format of the standardized test. It's not fair for me to always use performance-based assessments and then expect my students to be successful on a multiple choice test.

Don't forget two of the foundations of rigorous, differentiated instruction: all students master essential content and they do so at rigorous levels. If we effectively implement rigorous differentiation, we will lessen or negate this concern.

Time Management Tip
Whether you do this electronically or on paper, check off as you teach the standards. At the end of each month or grading period, take stock and make adjustments.

Homework

Should homework also be differentiated? What does that look like?

For this question, I turned to one of my former graduate students, Christy Matkovich. When she was working on her master's degree, she was a middle school math teacher, and she had a strong focus on differentiating her classroom. She shares two common misconceptions about differentiated homework.

There are two misconceptions about differentiated homework. The first one is the idea that varying the *amount* of homework each ability level receives is a good way to differentiate homework. In some classrooms, the scholars students receive 10 more problems than the low achieving students, and teachers justify it by saying, "If they are scholars level, then they should be able to handle a longer homework assignment." In other classrooms, the low achieving students receive 10 more problems. This practice is also justified by teachers claiming, "These students just need more practice before the concept will stick in their heads so they can remember how to do it." Neither one of these justifications make sense. If the scholars students already understand a concept, why must they waste their time repeating the process over and over again when they could be using that time to extend and expand their knowledge into new areas they have yet to explore? On the other hand, giving lower achievers 10 extra problems simply gives them the opportunity to practice a concept incorrectly 10 more times, giving you a much bigger challenge of reversing the effects of incorrectly practicing a concept.

The second misconception is the idea that varying the *quality* of the assignment is a good way to differentiate homework. An example of this misconception showed up in a sixth grade classroom. The class was working on adding, subtracting, multiplying, and dividing fractions. For homework one night, the higher achieving students received 10 word problems that contained fractions. These word problems related fractions to the different interests of the students. There were problems about sports, music, and other topics of interest. The students were to read the problems and then decide if they should add, subtract, multiply, or divide. After choosing an operation, they were to complete the problem and give their answer in a complete sentence. The lower achieving students were given 10 fraction problems out of the textbook. These problems were basic drill problems with two fractions and an operation. The students were to simply perform the operation and come up with the correct answer. The idea of providing lower level quality to some students is not reflective of a rigorous, differentiated classroom.

I asked Christy what she would tell a teacher who is just starting to differentiate homework. She has two tips.

Keeping It Manageable

♦ Keep in mind that you do not have to differentiate homework assignments every night to be effective. It's best to begin slowly to help students adjust to the differences and to help you manage your time.

♦ You do not have to design a different homework assignment for every child in the class. You can begin by creating two homework assignments, a higher level and a lower level, both with rigorous aspects.

Finally, she provided me with a set of steps to measure progress for incorporating differentiated homework. A minimal level of differentiation is at the bottom of stairs (step one), and you move up to complete implementation at the top (step four). She recommends setting a goal of moving up one step per year.

Ladder for Implementing Differentiation

Highest Level Implementation

I fully integrate information from students' learning portraits, pre-assessments, and ongoing formative assessments to provide support to students.

Our classroom norms are built around the concept of differentiated support. Although there are times when whole-class instruction is appropriate, a variety of groupings, including partners, small groups, and individual work, are used based on students' learning portraits and the assessments.

All students have a growth mindset.

Students have become more independent learners. They regularly ask for support when it is needed, but they regularly attempt work on their own or with others before asking the teacher for help.

All scaffolding and support leads to rigorous learning.

Step 4

I incorporate information from students' learning portraits, pre-assessments and ongoing formative assessments to determine support needs of all students.

Although I use general scaffolding with whole-group instruction, I regularly differentiate support for individuals and small groups of students,

We regularly discuss and practice growth mindset activities. Students, including those students who are focused on ability, are learning the importance of moving forward. Advanced students sometimes are willing to accept help.

All scaffolding and support ensures students move from where they are to a rigorous level of learning

Step 3

I have gathered information about students from their learning portraits. Before and during presentation of new information, I sometimes use formative assessment to determine how to differentiate the support students need.

I teach a variety of problem-solving strategies to all students in a whole-group session. Some of my students understand the concept of growth mindset and how effort impacts their learning.

At times, I use the specific scaffolding strategies I designed after formative assessment with individuals or small groups of students.

I attempt to use scaffolding that ensures students work toward a rigorous level of learning.

Step 2

Lowest Level Implementation

New information is presented primarily in lecture or a discussion format in a whole group setting.

I use general support. I teach students standard ways to take notes, solve word problems, etc. All of my students must use what I showed them at the beginning of the year. This way everyone is using the same method.

Most of my students have a fixed mindset.

If students need extra help to be successful, they can stay after school for help.

For struggling students, I usually make the work easier so they can be successful.

Step 1

Grading

What About Grading?

Grading was another challenge for me, and grading in a differentiated classroom is particularly difficult for students with special needs and those who are gifted. Let's start by looking at students with special needs or those who are struggling. Common questions include: "How can we ensure rigorous grading without defeating students if they don't meet the standards? Should I grade effort? What should count and how do I grade that?"

These are difficult questions, and I do not have a perfect solution. Ideally, we would use report cards that allow us to put two grades: one that represents how they perform compared to the grade level standards and one that shows how they are performing at their level. Unfortunately, many districts do not allow for this. So, what are our alternatives?

Thomas Guskey, in *Practical Solutions for Serious Problems in Standards-Based Grading*, suggests five categories that allow you to customize a grading system to meet individual needs in a standards-based system.

Five Categories to Customize Standards-Based Grading System
1. Considering progress on IEP goals
2. Measuring improvement over past performance
3. Prioritizing assignments or content differently
4. Including indicators or behavior effort in the grade
5. Modifying the weight or skill for grading

Teachers like this process, because it helps students feel successful when they otherwise might not. However, students may misinterpret their grades, believing they haven't earned them; they simply received a grade for who they are.

Based on those concerns, let's look at a second model by Jung and Thomas Guskey. This is designed to allow classroom teachers and special needs teachers to work together to grade in a standards-based environment.

> ### *Five-Step Inclusive Grading Model*
> 1. Determine if the accommodations or modifications are needed for each grade-level standard
> 2. Establish the appropriate modified standard for each area requiring modification
> 3. Outline additional goals pertinent to the child's academic success
> 4. Apply equal grading practices to the appropriate standards
> 5. Clearly communicate grades' meanings

In this five-step inclusive grading model, students are still measured to the standards, but with appropriate accommodations and modifications for the student.

Grading students with special needs is challenging, and ultimately, you must work with other teachers in your school, including the teacher of special needs students to determine the best way to grade within your school's, district's, and state's parameters. This is also true as you work with grading other struggling learners.

Differentiating grading for gifted students is another challenging area, one for which there are no clear solutions. You might follow some of the same strategies as for special needs students (i.e., customizing the grade, noting on the report card where they are based on grade level standards and what they score compared to more rigorous standards). Although not a solution, there are two key questions for you to consider as you grade gifted students:

1. Do students show mastery of grade level standards as well as more rigorous standards?
2. Are you clearly communicating to the student and parents/families what the student is and is not able to do?

No matter where your students are on the learning spectrum, your main goal in a rigorous, differentiated classroom is to provide all students opportunities to demonstrate their learning of essential skills, albeit in different ways. Your grading should reflect that goal.

Gifted and Advanced Learners

I'm so focused on tiering instruction for my struggling learners, I'm afraid I'm neglecting my students who are gifted or advanced. Do you have any suggestions?

This is another concern that I dealt with as a teacher. My struggling students had so many needs, it seemed that I just didn't have anything left for my gifted or advanced students. Please note that I understand the differences between those who are identified as gifted and talented, and those students who are simply working at advanced levels. However, these suggestions are applicable to both groups.

First, intentionally plan your tierings to include gifted and advanced students. You might plan this tier first, so you can give it your full attention (before you become tired!). Next, be sure your plans do not focus on increasing quantity of work. Too often, we give our advanced students a worksheet with 10 extra problems that are harder. That is absolutely a mistake. It doesn't enhance learning, and students feel as though they are being punished. Instead, follow the recommendations I've provided to provide more complex work that is appropriate.

Next, take time regularly, whether it is weekly, monthly, or quarterly, to review your standards and identify ones that are appropriate for curriculum compacting (see Chapter 3 for more information). Curriculum compacting is one of your most effective tools for meeting the needs of gifted and advanced students. The National Association for Gifted Children provides data to support the use of curriculum compacting.

Rationale for Using Curriculum Compacting With Gifted Students

◆ Elementary teachers can eliminate 24–70% of high-ability students' curriculum by compacting without any negative effect on test scores or performance. In fact, curriculum compacting can

---

have a positive effect on students' performance. Because many talented students receive little differentiation of instruction from their peers, they spend a great deal of time in school doing work that they have already mastered. Curriculum compacting allows these students to avoid having to relearn material they already know, which research has shown can lead to frustration, boredom, and, ultimately, underachievement.

♦ Researchers have reported that when classroom teachers eliminated between 40% and 50% of the previously mastered regular curriculum for high-ability students, no differences were found between students whose work was compacted and students who did all of the work in reading, math computation, social studies, and spelling. In an analysis of gifted education literature on the topic, another researcher found curriculum compacting to be very effective overall in mathematics, science, and foreign languages.

♦ In a national study of curriculum compacting, the students who received compacting in science and mathematics actually scored significantly higher on achievement posttests than their peers in the control group, suggesting the benefits of compacting for increases on standard achievement assessments. Analyses of data related to students' thoughts about replacement activities indicated that the students viewed the new curricular options as much more challenging than standard material.

Source: http://nagc.org/resources-publications/gifted-education-practices/curriculum-compacting

Finally, simply be intentional about your desire to address the needs of your gifted students. Choose to make it a priority, make sure it is on your to-do list, and take action.

Time Management Tip
Incorporate addressing the needs of gifted and talented into your planning. This ensures you won't forget.

Differentiation, Personalization, and Individualization

My school is focusing on personalization of learning, and I have a friend who talks about individualization. How do those relate to differentiation?

I can understand why you are confused. I've talked with teachers and leaders who use the terms interchangeably. Although there are similarities, there are specific differences. In their article, *Building Personalized Learning Environments*, Barbara Bray and Kathleen McClaskey compare the three.

Personalization vs. Differentiation vs. Individualization Chart (v3)

Personalization	Differentiation	Individualization
The Learner . . .	*The Teacher . . .*	*The Teacher . . .*
Drives their learning.	Provides instruction to groups of learners.	Provides instruction to an individual learner.
Connects learning with interests, talents, passions, and aspirations.	Adjusts learning needs for groups of learners.	Accommodates learning needs for the individual learner.
Actively participates in the design of their learning.	Designs instruction based on the learning needs of different groups of learners.	Customizes instruction based on the learning needs of the individual learner.
Owns and is responsible for their learning that includes their voice and choice on how and what they learn.	Is responsible for a variety of instruction for different groups of learners.	Is responsible for modifying instruction based on the needs of the individual learner.

Personalization	Differentiation	Individualization
The Learner . . .	*The Teacher . . .*	*The Teacher . . .*
Identifies goals for their learning plan and benchmarks as they progress along their learning path with guidance from teacher.	Identifies the same objectives for different groups of learners as they do for the whole class.	Identifies the same objectives for all learners with specific objectives for individuals who receive one-on-one support.
Acquires the skills to select and use the appropriate technology and resources to support and enhance their learning.	Selects technology and resources to support the learning needs of different groups of learners.	Selects technology and resources to support the learning needs of the individual learner.
Builds a network of peers, experts, and teachers to guide and support their learning.	Supports groups of learners who are reliant on them for their learning.	Understands the individual learner is dependent on them to support their learning.
Demonstrates mastery of content in a competency-based system.	Monitors learning based on Carnegie unit (seat time) and grade level.	Monitors learning based on Carnegie unit (seat time) and grade level.
Becomes a self-directed, expert learner who monitors progress and reflects on learning based on mastery of content and skills.	Uses data and assessments to modify instruction for groups of learners and provides feedback to individual learners to advance learning.	Uses data and assessments to measure progress of what the individual learner learned and did not learn to decide next steps in their learning.

(Continued)

(Continued)

Personalization	Differentiation	Individualization
The Learner . . .	*The Teacher* . . .	*The Teacher* . . .
Assessment AS and FOR Learning with minimal OF Learning	Assessment OF and FOR Learning	Assessment OF Learning

 Personalization vs. Differentiation vs. Individualization Chart (v3) by Barbara Bray & Kathleen McClaskey Version 3 is licensed under a Creative CommonsAttribution-NonCommercial-NoDerivs 3.0 Unported License. For permission to use or distribute copies, contact Barbara Bray at barbara.bray@gmail.com or Kathleen McClaskey at khmcclaskey@gmail.com

Credit line: by Barbara Bray & Kathleen McClaskey Used with permission. Version 3 is licensed under a Creative CommonsAttribution-NonCommercial-NoDerivs 3.0 Unported License. For permission to use or distribute copies, contact Barbara Bray at barbara.bray@gmail.com or Kathleen McClaskey at khmcclaskey@gmail.com

Source: www.advanc-ed.org/source/building-personalized-learning-environments

I disagree with the language in some points, such as the idea that differentiation focuses only on groups of students. In an effective differentiated classroom, individuals are also supported as needed. I also believe that in a differentiated classroom, you can provide opportunities for students to drive their own learning. Of note, the authors tend to lean toward personalization as the best model, which is to be expected since they own a company that focuses on personalized learning.

Communicating With Parents and Families

What information should I share with parents and families? I would like them to understand what we are doing because it is different.

Communicating with parents and other family members is a critical part of your successful implementation of a rigorous, differentiated classroom. It's important to use a variety of methods to share information, including email, websites, social media, newsletters, and meetings. There are two types of information you should share with parents and families.

> **Types of Information to Share**
>
> Share what is happening in the classroom.
>
> Share how parents and families can help.

Share What Is Happening in the Classroom

Begin by explaining to parents and families what they can expect to hear their sons and daughters are doing in class. In other words, what are some examples of how the classroom works?

> **Examples of Classroom Practices**
>
> ♦ I'll be learning as much as I can about your son or daughter so that I can help them learn.
>
> ♦ Sometimes we will be learning as an entire class; other times students will work in small groups or individually.
>
> ♦ Instruction will include questions that require thinking and they may have more than one answer (give samples appropriate to grade levels and subjects).
>
> ♦ When they answer a question, students will be asked to show where they found the answer in the story/article/text.
>
> ♦ They'll be using problem-solving in all subjects, not just memorizing facts.
>
> ♦ On their homework, they will be asked to explain their answers.
>
> ♦ If something is too easy, I'll move your son/daughter to more rigorous work, probably in a small group, so they will be challenged.
>
> ♦ If something is too hard, I'll provide extra help to your son or daughter, perhaps in a small group, so that he or she can still accomplish high levels of learning.
>
> ♦ There will be times when different students or groups of students will be doing different things. This doesn't mean some students will be "punished" with more work; rather, I'll be customizing some lessons and assignments so that each student will be successful.
>
> ♦ At times, students will be able to choose what they are doing, based on their interests.

Create standard parent communications as a school, then customize by grade level, team, or department.

Share How They Can Help

Next, provide concrete, specific strategies they can use to help support their son or daughter's learning.

Rigor and Differentiation Tip Sheet for Parents

1. Rigor is helping your son or daughter think for him or herself. You can help your son or daughter do this by teaching him or her to think beyond the text, by asking questions starting with "What if . . ."

2. Rigor is helping your son or daughter make connections among the disciplines. Ask, "How does this topic relate to what you are studying in your other classes?"

3. Rigor is encouraging students to provide their own answers to questions. When your son or daughter asks for help, provide guidance, not answers. Too much help teaches that someone will do the work for him or her.

4. Rigor is providing a supportive environment at home for your son or daughter to work. Students need to know it is okay if their answers are not perfect and that they can ask for help as long as they have exhausted other measures, such as checking class notes, looking to the text or other reading material, or doing some light research online.

5. Because we are differentiating instruction, sometimes your son or daughter will be doing something different from a friend. Be positive and help your son or daughter understand that doing something different is what is best for his or her learning; it's not punishment for being "too dumb" or "too smart."

6. Also be understanding and supportive of the different groups that students will be in. Sometimes, your son or daughter may be worried that they are not in the "right group." Communicate with me so you can understand what is happening, and then encourage your son or daughter to do their best.

---

7. Help me learn as much as I can about your son or daughter. The more I know, the more I can help him or her.

8. Don't hesitate to contact me to discuss any concerns. We are using some new strategies that definitely work, but they are different. I want you to know that, together, we can help your son or daughter be successful.

Working With Leaders

Even though my principal told us that we were expected to differentiate our classrooms while retaining the level of rigor for learning, she doesn't really provide any support. For example, all the teachers asked for professional development, and she gave us a book to read. We want to visit other schools so we can talk to teachers who are further along on the journey, but she says we can't afford it. We've asked for more planning time, and she says we will just have to make do. Can you give me any advice?

It's clear that you are in a tough situation, one in which you are asked to do something with little to no help. I'm always disappointed when I hear questions such as this because they don't reveal the behaviors of an effective instructional leader. However, there are times when this is your reality, and we need to address it.

I'd start with what you have, which is the book your principal provided (hopefully it contains quality information). Rather than each teacher simply reading it, meet in small groups (perhaps grade levels, teams, or departments) and discuss what you learned. Then, share ideas that you can try to implement in your classrooms. Even though this requires time, try to fit it into existing meetings, rather than scheduling another time to get together. For example, if your grade level meets every other Monday for an hour for planning, carve out the first 15 minutes to discuss the book.

Next, choose a few teachers who have a good relationship with your principal, and ask them to set up a time to talk with her. Start with the positive.

We wanted to start by letting you know that everyone has really enjoyed reading the book you provided. We discussed what we learned in small groups, and shared ideas. It was very helpful as a starting point, and we are beginning to understand what to do.

Next, transition into what you need. Limit your requests so that your principal is not overwhelmed, and research options before the conversation to provide a plan, so she is more likely to supply what you need.

We know this is important to you, and we want to be successful, but we need some additional support. We have a couple of ideas we would like to discuss with you. First, we found that sharing ideas with each other was helpful, but it would be nice to hear ideas from everyone in the school, not just our grade level. When you are planning our hour-long faculty meetings, would you schedule 10 minutes at the beginning to allow us to share ideas? The grade level chairs are willing to coordinate the schedule and make sure we stay on time.

Next, we believe it would be very important to see classrooms in other schools and talk with teachers who have already implemented rigorous differentiation. If we can do this, we'll be able to avoid some common mistakes. We've done some research and identified two schools that are similar to ours within a two-hour drive. We understand that budgets are tight, so we thought you might be able to let four teachers visit each school. That would mean we would take one car, and we would not need to stay overnight. We could eat at the school, so our lunch would be inexpensive. One of the schools runs on a different schedule, so we could visit it on our next workday. That would save money on substitute teachers. We are also willing to prepare a proposal to ask for the funding from the Parent-Teacher Association.

Notice how in this scenario, you come to the table with a detailed plan, one that reinforces the positive action she has already taken (providing a book) and explaining why you need the support (to implement her plan). Finally, you asked for very specific activities and provided a plan for accomplishing it. You anticipated possible obstacles (funding) and addressed those in advance. This should increase your opportunity to get the needed support.

One observation from my experience with schools that do not have strong leadership from their building administrators is that this allows for teachers to grow in their own leadership skills. Work together as a faculty to share responsibilities and make the best of a bad situation. Finally, recognize and accept that progress toward implementation may be slower.

A Final Note

When differentiating rigorous instruction, you may encounter some challenges. Incorporate these lessons learned from other teachers to help you succeed.

 Points to Ponder

The most important thing I learned was . . .
I was surprised about . . .
I want to learn more about . . .
I'd like to try . . .

8

Leading Change for Rigor in the Differentiated Classroom

In their book, *Differentiation for Gifted and Talented Students*, Carol Ann Tomlinson and Sally Reis describe conclusions from a set of case studies. They found there were six common themes across the schools that led to successful implementations of differentiated instruction.

Themes

Teachers' advanced knowledge and training

Teachers' willingness and readiness to embrace change

Collaboration

Teachers' beliefs and strategies for differentiating curriculum

Leadership

Autonomy and support

I've found that, although teacher leadership is a strong aspect of any initiative, change typically begins with and is supported by strong administrative leadership. This does not demean the role of teachers; it simply acknowledges that a strong administrator who provides leadership, autonomy, and support can drive positive change.

The other four themes—teachers' advanced knowledge and training, teachers' willingness and readiness to embrace change, collaboration, teachers' beliefs and strategies for differentiating curriculum—are influenced by ongoing professional development activities. This may include attending conferences and interactive workshops, but for the most impact, continuing, job-embedded activities work best. Much of this can occur through professional learning communities (PLCs).

Professional Learning Communities

Many teachers are members of professional learning communities. The term has become so commonplace that it can mean any type of collaboration.

The original meaning of a professional community of learners reflected the commitment of teachers and leaders who continuously seek to grow professionally and act upon their new learning.

Options for Professional Learning Communities

Interdisciplinary Teams

Subject Area Teams

Grade Level Teams

Special Topic Teams

Vertical Teams

There are three defining characteristics of PLCs. First, professional learning communities are focused on student learning. As Richard DuFour and his colleagues (2016) note, the goal is to improve student learning by improving what you do in the classroom.

Next, there is a culture of collaboration among the participants. You've probably worked in or seen a team of teachers who were assigned to a task, each performed their part of the task, and then they walked away. That's not a true PLC. In a PLC, teachers collaborate to move beyond tasks and learn together.

Finally, professional learning communities focus on results, no matter what it takes. Although there may be a discussion of challenges, they are not used as excuses.

Successful professional learning communities provide time for you and other teachers to talk about curriculum and instruction, examine data about student learning, and plan for instructional improvements. For instance, when implementing rigorous activities that are differentiated, it is helpful to discuss ideas with other teachers, receive feedback, and then work together to plan the best implementation.

Time Management Tip

 Professional learning communities do not need to be "another thing to do." It is simply another way to think about how you work together with other teachers. Don't necessarily try to find another block of time for a PLC; see if you can adjust current meeting times for PLC activities.

Benefits and Challenges of Collaboration and Shared Decision-Making

Collaboration is the most critical aspect of improving our instructional practices, and it is a critical part of a PLC. There are many benefits, but there are also some challenges. The challenges should not keep you from moving forward; you simply need to address them in a positive manner.

Benefits	Challenges
• Higher-quality decisions because more perspectives are considered • Increased job satisfaction and morale • Heightened sense of empowerment • Greater ownership of goals and priorities when participants have a stake in the decision • Improved student achievement because of greater coordination of work among stakeholders	• Expanded participation may require more time to make decisions • Group dynamics may stifle ideas, leading to "groupthink" • Polarization around specific points of view • People feeling left out or that some have greater access and opportunity to influence decisions

Norms of Collaboration

In any collaborative process, it's important to have agreed-upon norms. Without them, the process can deteriorate into personal attacks or an off-task discussion. Robert Garmston and Bruce Wellman (2013) have created a set of seven norms of collaboration.

Seven Norms of Collaboration

1. **Pausing**: Pausing before responding or asking a question allows time for thinking and enhances dialogue, discussion, and decision making.

2. **Paraphrasing**: Using a paraphrase starter that is comfortable for you, such as "As you are saying . . . " or "You're thinking . . . " and following the starter with a paraphrase assists members of the group to hear and understand each other as they formulate decisions.

3. **Probing**: Using gentle open-ended probes or inquiries such as, "Please say more . . . " or "I'm curious about . . . " or "I'd like to hear more about . . . " or "Then, are you saying . . . ?" increases the clarity and precision of the group's thinking.

4. **Putting ideas on the table**: Ideas are the heart of a meaningful dialogue. Label the intention of your comments. For example, you might say, "Here is one idea . . . " or "One thought I have is . . . " or "Here is a possible approach . . . "

5. **Paying attention to self and others**: Meaningful dialogue is facilitated when each group member is conscious of self and of others and is aware of not only what he or she is saying but also how it is said and how others are responding. This includes paying attention to learning style when planning for, facilitating, and participating in group meetings.

6. **Presuming positive intentions**: Assuming that others' intentions are positive promotes and facilitates meaningful dialogue and eliminates unintentional put-downs. Using positive intentions in your speech is one manifestation of this norm.

7. **Pursuing a balance between advocacy and inquiry**: Pursuing and maintaining a balance between advocating a position and inquiring about one's own and others' positions assists the group to become a learning organization.

Source: Garmston and Wellman (2013)

Time Management Tip

In addition to following protocols such as those described above, have an agenda for PLC meetings and follow it. If someone isn't on time, start without him or her. End on time, unless everyone in the group agrees that you need to continue. If you don't follow a schedule, it's easy to get off track, not accomplish your goals, and waste time.

Activities for Professional Learning Communities

Although there are many ways for PLCs to work together, we are going to take a look at five that can help you maximize your efforts to improve the rigor and differentiation in your classroom.

Five Activities for Professional Learning Communities
1. Develop Consistent Expectations
2. Learning Walks
3. Lesson Studies
4. Charrettes
5. Self-Reflection to Gauge Progress

Develop Consistent Expectations

One activity that is particularly beneficial when used in a PLC is for teachers to work together to develop consistent expectations, both in terms of rigor and differentiation. For example, you can bring examples of differentiated tasks, assignments, and projects that require students to demonstrate understanding and assess them to determine the level of rigor based on Webb's Depth of Knowledge levels. Below, you will see a partial set of guiding questions teachers can use to collaboratively assess tasks, projects, and assignments.

It's important that the discussion is focused on results, not on personalities. At the beginning of the process, agree on a process for the discussion. One way to discuss the positive and challenging aspects of a task, project, or assignment is to adapt a student feedback form for writing. Discuss what makes an assignment "glow" and where an assignment needs to "grow."

Time Management Tip
As with any PLC activity, detail a series of specific steps to follow to accomplish your goal. This will keep you on track and help you not waste time.

Webb's DOK Level 1	*Webb's DOK Level 2*	*Webb's DOK Level 3*	*Webb's DOK Level 4*
• Are you asking a fact-based or basic recall question? • Does it require basic comprehension? • Does it lack higher order thinking skills? • Does the assessment require simply following basic instructions?	• Are students processing texts for analysis or inference? • Does it include basic application of material? • Are students taking notes or writing a simple summary? • Are students interpreting basic information from a graphic?	• Does the assessment focus on deeper knowledge? • Do students go beyond the text information, while demonstrating they understand the text? • Are students encouraged to explain, generalize, or connect ideas? • Is there more than one possible response? • Are students required to explain or justify their response? • Are students recognizing and explaining misconceptions?	• Are the cognitive demands high and the work very complex? • Is the response typically an extended one that requires additional time? Is it at least a level 3 of complexity but it takes more time? • Are students required to make several connections—relate ideas *within* the content area or *among* content areas—and have to select one approach among many alternatives on how the situation should be solved, in order to be at this highest level?

Learning Walks

Learning walks, which are 5- to 10-minute classroom visits, provide a "snapshot" of what is happening in classrooms. They are not used for evaluative purposes or for individual feedback; rather, their purpose is to help teachers learn about overall instruction. Additionally, the goal is to identify areas of instructional strengths and possible challenges.

Members of the PLC should plan the focus of the walks, which include looking for overall patterns within a grade level, subject area, or school. You may also want to begin with only looking for positive examples, in order to build trust.

A school in Chicago organized "I Spy" days. Teachers dropped in on classrooms for 5 to 10 minutes in order to identify positive examples of instruction. Teachers came back together after school with their "detective notebooks" to share what they had seen. It was an invigorating experience for teachers, who said this was the first time they had a chance to look at other classrooms. As one teacher explained, "I don't get time to visit other teachers' classes. I learned so much, and I have two new ideas I want to implement tomorrow."

You may also want to use a short tool to help teachers guide note-taking during the mini-observations.

Taking Notes During Observations

Grade Level	Subject
This was the best thing I saw: _100_	I learned:
I have a question about: **?**	Other Notes:

Lesson Studies

Lesson studies emphasize working in small groups to plan, teach, observe, and critique a lesson. It's an excellent reflection of the principles of professional learning communities, as the goal is to systematically examine your teaching in order to become more effective.

In a lesson study, teachers work together to develop or adapt an existing lesson into a detailed rigorous differentiated plan for a lesson. One member of the group teaches the lesson to his or her students while other members of the group observe. Next, the group discusses their observations about the lesson and student learning.

Teachers revise the lesson based on their observations, then a second group member teaches the lesson, with other members once again observing. Then, the group meets to discuss the revised lesson. Finally, teachers talk about what the study lesson taught them and how they can apply the learning in their own classroom.

Charrettes

A "charrette" is a set of agreed-upon guidelines for talking with colleagues about an issue. The conversation tends to be more trusting and more substantive because everyone knows the guidelines in advance. Charrettes are often used to improve the work while the work is in progress and are not to be used as an evaluative tool. Additional information about the charrette process is available at http://schoolreforminitiative. org/doc/charrette.pdf.

Charrette Protocol

1. A group or an individual from the group requests a charrette when they want others to help them resolve an issue. Often they are at a "sticking point" and the conversation will help them move forward.

2. Another small group is invited to look at the work and a facilitator is used to moderate the discussion.

3. The requesting group or individual presents its work and states what they need or want from the discussion. The conversation is focused by this presentation.

4. The invited group discusses the issue and the requesting group listens and takes notes. The emphasis is on improving the work, which now belongs to the entire group. "We're in this together" characterizes the discussion.

5. Once the requesting group gets what it needs, it stops the process, summarizes what was learned, thanks participants, and returns to their work.

Adapted From: "Charrette Protocol," written by Kathy Juarez and available on the *School Reform Initiative* website (http://schoolreforminitiative.org/doc/charrette.pdf)

Time Management Tip

Charettes are best used when one or more teachers are struggling with an issue. However, often teachers will veer off-topic into other concerns. Stay focused, or it will take too much time.

Self-Reflection to Gauge Progress

One of the most frustrating aspects of teaching is determining whether you are making progress toward your goal of rigorous, differentiated instruction. It's easy to decide that what you are doing isn't working when you have a bad day (or two). Instead, use the rubric below to gauge growth.

I would recommend that you start by reflecting on each point individually, considering where you believe you are in your current practice. Then, in your PLC, you and your colleagues can discuss, in general terms, where you might initiate change, both in your personal classrooms, and within your PLC as a group. Be specific with your action steps and remember to start small so you don't become overwhelmed.

Revisit the rubric periodically, perhaps once per month or once per grading period, to identify areas of growth, determine how to adjust your current efforts, and decide on next steps.

Rubric for Gauging Progress Toward Rigor and Differentiation

	Starting at the Base	Making Progress Up the Mountain	Reaching New Heights
Overall Classroom Environment	• Members of our learning community (students, teachers, parents, etc.) are learning what it means to meet the needs of all students through differentiation. • Parents are concerned that rigor will be lessened for students that are not advanced or gifted. • I sometimes adjust my instruction and routines for some to ensure a rigorous, differentiated classroom.	• Some members of our learning community (students, teachers, parents, etc.) believe that we must meet the needs of all students through differentiation. • Parents have a basic understanding that differentiation will help their sons and daughters, no matter their skill level. • The majority of the time, I am adjusting my instruction and routines to ensure a rigorous, differentiated classroom for many of my students.	• All or most members of our learning community (students, teachers, parents, etc.) are committed to ensuring that we meet the needs of all students through differentiation. • Parents and students regularly see progress in learning and are confident that each student is learning at high levels. • My standard instruction and routines ensure a rigorous, differentiated classroom for all students.

| Learning Portraits | <ul><li>I understand what a learning portrait is and I am collecting basic information on each student.</li><li>If a student is struggling, I look at their information, particularly their test scores, to see if it can help me understand what I need to do.</li><li>I sometimes group my struggling students based on their low test scores so I can provide basic instruction.</li></ul> | <ul><li>I have built a standard learning portrait for each student that, while it contains standardized testing information, also includes information on a variety of other factors to provide a fuller picture of each student.</li><li>If a student is struggling, I look at their information (test scores and additional information) to see if it can help me understand what I need to do.</li><li>I sometimes group my students based on aspects of their learning portraits, more than just test scores.</li></ul> | <ul><li>I have built extensive learning portraits for each student that contain detailed information that provides a complete picture of each student.</li><li>I refer to the learning portraits as I plan my lessons to ensure success for each student.</li><li>I revisit the learning portraits as needed during my instruction to supplement instruction.</li><li>The learning portraits, as well as formative assessments, guide my student groupings.</li></ul> |

(Continued)

Expectations	Starting at the Base	Making Progress Up the Mountain	Reaching New Heights
	• I post the objectives for students, or I clearly state them in terms they can understand. I create and implement lessons that are clearly aligned with the objectives. • My lessons provide some general differentiation, especially asking different questions. • Every once in a while, I pull a small group of students for specialized instruction. Students sometimes perceive this negatively. • I pay attention to the rigor of my instruction, especially incorporating higher order questions in our discussions, but most of my activities are at Level 2 of Webb's Depth of Knowledge.	• Students understand the objectives, and they see how the lesson(s) relate. • I am beginning to use some differentiated options, such as providing tiered instruction or compacting the curriculum. • Tiered instruction includes regularly working with a variety of groups. Because the members of the groups are adjusted based on changing needs, there is not a stigma to needing extra assistance, which helps students learn. • Through tiered instruction, I am working to incorporate rigorous activities, especially those at Level 3 of Webb's Depth of Knowledge, for all students, some of whom demonstrate understanding at those rigorous levels.	• Students thoroughly understand and share ownership of learning related to the objectives. • Tiered instruction and compacting the curriculum are a standard part of my instruction, and my students thrive in the differentiated environment. • Flexible groupings occur regularly, are based on a variety of factors in addition to readiness, and help students thrive. • Through standard and tiered instruction, I regularly provide rigorous activities, especially those at Levels 3 and 4 of Webb's Depth of Knowledge, for all students who are able to master the rigorous work.

| Support and Scaffolding | • I provide general support during my instruction, which should allow students to succeed.
• I choose my support strategies based on what I have used in the past.
• Students who need extra help can meet with me individually, whether after school or at another time. | • Although I provide general support, I also provide some scaffolding for individual students and small groups.
• I choose my support strategies based in part on what I have used in the past, but considering my current students, not assuming they are the same as former students. I look for new strategies when those don't work.
• I make sure that students are provided some support during class, in recognition of the fact that some students who need help won't ask for it or stay after school. | • Whole group, small group, and individual scaffolding and support is woven throughout my instruction to ensure success for all students.
• I choose my support strategies based on those that have been proven successful in the past, the learning portraits of my students, and new strategies that have been shown to be effective.
• I make sure that students are provided the support they need to be successful. That may include extra time outside of class, such as time after school, but I provide an alternative that students without transportation can attend. |

(Continued)

(Continued)

	Starting at the Base	Making Progress Up the Mountain	Reaching New Heights
Demonstration of Learning	• When I'm teaching a new lesson, I try to incorporate characteristics of quality, rigorous assignments. • Sometimes I revise my existing lessons to incorporate characteristics of quality, rigorous assignments. • I'm improving my tests and performance-based assignments so they will be rigorous, at Levels 3 and 4 of Webb's Depth of Knowledge. Many of them are at Level 1, so I am usually able to move them to Level 2. • I use the same test or performance-based assignment with all students, but I allow them to relate certain test answers to their own experiences or interests.	• When I'm teaching a new lesson, I sometimes create and implement quality, rigorous assignments. • I always review my existing lessons to incorporate characteristics of quality, rigorous assignments, and I make appropriate revisions. • I'm improving my tests and performance-based assignments so they will be rigorous, at Levels 3 and 4 of Webb's Depth of Knowledge, but many of them are at Level 2, so I am sometimes able to move them to Level 3. • I generally use the same test or performance-based assignment with all students, but I do try to differentiate them at times, generally based on skill level, or perhaps interest.	• My lessons consistently incorporate quality, rigorous assignments—whether they are newly designed lessons or those I have revised. • Because of my revisions to existing lessons and new lessons I have created, my tests and performance-based assignments are usually at Levels 3 and 4 of Webb's Depth of Knowledge, but I use Level 1 or 2 activities as needed to build to Levels 3 and 4. • I differentiate tests based on a variety of factors from students' learning portraits, as well as formative assessments, in ways that ensure student success.

• For performance-based assignments, I allow some choice. For example, instead of writing an essay about a historical figure, they can create a video, write a blog, create a fake Facebook page, or design a brochure.	• I do adjust performance-based assignments for students, especially based on readiness or interest. For example, I provide more rigorous assignments to my advanced students, and I do try to provide rigorous assignments for my struggling students.	• I regularly adjust performance-based assignments for students, based on their learning portraits and formative assessment. No matter their readiness or skill level, students are provided opportunities to be successful with rigorous work.

Becoming a Teacher-Leader

As you consider the ideas we have discussed, you'll see that being a teacher-leader is at the heart of instructional change. You may already be a teacher-leader, even if you don't realize it.

In 2015, BloomBoard conducted research with the Council for Chief State School Officers. Three of their findings inform our conversation about becoming a teacher-leader.

Three Key Findings

1. 92% of states surveyed reported that teachers have opportunity for leadership as curriculum specialists, but only 9% of teachers report serving in this role.

2. 92% of states surveyed reported that teachers have opportunity for leadership as mentors, but only 18% of teachers report serving in this role.

3. Most states said teachers have a variety of formal and informal leadership opportunities, but not many teachers reported acting as leaders.

Source: http://blog.bloomboard.com/understanding-teacher-leadership-opportunities-5-ideas-for-action

This tells us there are opportunities for teachers to also be leaders, but that many teachers do not take advantage of those opportunities. This may be due to time and other responsibilities, but it is often because many of us don't realize that we can be instructional leaders.

Cindy Harrison and Joellen Killion, in their article *Ten Roles for Teacher Leaders*, provide ideas for the types of roles you might engage in as a teacher-leader. I have one caution for you. In many schools, there are personnel who are designated in one of these roles, such as instructional specialist. Therefore, you may feel you cannot take on that role. However, you can—just in a different way. An instructional specialist, for example, can be someone who works with other teachers to design innovative lesson plans. Or it can be someone who researches a topic and shares that with other teachers. Do not feel limited by a title.

Ten Roles for Teacher-Leaders

1. Resource Provider
2. Instructional Specialist
3. Curriculum Specialist

---

4. Classroom Supporter

5. Learning Facilitator

6. Mentor

7. School Leader

8. Data Coach

9. Catalyst for Change

10. Learner

Source: www.ascd.org/publications/educational-leadership/
sept07/vol65/num01/Ten-Roles-for-Teacher-Leaders.aspx

How can you move into a teacher-leader role? First, understand what it means to be a teacher-leader. Next, reflect on what you do and consider whether or not you are a teacher-leader already and whether you want to be one. Finally, look for opportunities, both formal and informal, where you can be a teacher-leader.

Some easy ways to start are to share ideas with another teacher, to lead a book study with other interested teachers, to research a topic and share it with teachers in a PLC, or to help a new teacher (even if you are not assigned as a mentor). Ultimately, teacher-leaders recognize they have something to contribute to the larger school community, and they act on that belief. If you are passionate about rigor and differentiation, act on your enthusiasm and become a teacher-leader.

Time Management Tip

Balance your enthusiasm about taking on a leadership role with your other responsibilities. Don't overcommit yourself. It's better to do a few things well than many things poorly.

Addressing Challenges

There are a variety of concerns teachers have about rigor and differentiation in the classroom. Although we have discussed strategies to deal with possible obstacles throughout this book, I'd like to take a moment in this chapter to refocus on those issues with a different lens. In the table below, you will find six common objections to implementing rigorous, differentiated instruction. Then you will find ideas to address the issues while working with other teachers, as well as a reference to the chapter in this book with supporting information.

Addressing Common Objections

Issue/Challenge	Ideas for Addressing Issue/Challenge	Chapter(s) in This Book With Supporting Information and Ideas
I don't know how.	Workshop on the basics of rigor and differentiation. Do a book study with discussion. Watch videos of rigorous, differentiated lessons. Ask other teachers in the school to share what they are doing that works. Visit other schools that have successfully implemented rigorous, differentiated instruction.	Chapters 2–8
This may work for other people, but they don't understand my students.	Visit other schools with similar student populations that have successfully implemented rigorous, differentiated instruction. Find and share stories of similar students who have been successful in a rigorous, differentiated classroom. Help teachers identify and/or adapt strategies that will be most effective with their students.	Chapters 2–8
My students' test scores are high. Why do I need to change?	Working together, complete a data analysis of test scores and identify students or groups of students who are not achieving as they should. This may be high achievers who do not show a full year's growth, or low achievers who did not make any progress. Discuss these patterns, as well as any needed changes. Find a school/schools with similar populations whose test scores exceed yours, especially in particular areas. Use this information to spark a discussion about needed changes.	Chapters 1, 2, 3, and 6

If I do this, my classroom is going to be chaotic. Won't my principal score me lower on my evaluation?	Ask other teachers in the school to share what they are doing that ensures effective classroom management. Visit other schools that have mastered effective classroom management in a rigorous, differentiated instruction. Use a book study or workshop to learn new strategies. School leadership should discuss expectations for observations with teachers, including the fact that purposeful student movement is not negative.	Chapters 6 and 7
How do I handle grading? Parents are going to be upset.	Ask other teachers in this school and other schools to share what they are doing that works. Use a book study or workshop to learn new strategies. Work together to develop and implement common, consistent grading policies. Using a plan designed by teachers and leaders, communicate regularly with parents.	Chapter 7
I don't have enough time to do everything now. This is one more thing. How do you expect me to have time?	Ask other teachers in this school and other schools to share what they are doing that works. Use a book study or workshop to learn new strategies. Focus on collaborative planning with grade levels, teams, or departments to reduce duplication of work. Work with school and district leaders to provide "protected" time to work on rigorous, differentiated instruction.	Chapters 6 and 7

A Final Note

In order to truly incorporate rigor and differentiation in schools, teachers must work together in a variety of ways that allow them to reflect on their own practices, learn about new practices, and share the successes and struggles as they implement change. Professional learning communities, supported by school and district leadership, can ensure progress toward your goals.

Points to Ponder

The most important thing I learned was . . .
I was surprised about . . .
I want to learn more about . . .
I'd like to try . . .

Bibliography

Allen, J. (2004). *Tools for teaching academic vocabulary*. Portland, ME: Stenhouse.

Ames, R., & Ames, C. (1990). Motivation and effective teaching. In B. F. Jones and L. Idol (eds.), *Dimensions of thinking and cognitive instruction*. Hillsdale, NJ: ErIbaum.

Bellanca, J., & Fogarty, R. (2003). *Blueprints for thinking in the cooperative classroom* (3rd edition). Glenview, IL: Pearson/Skylight.

Bender, W. N. (2009). *Differentiating math Instruction: Strategies that work for K–8 classrooms*. Thousand Oaks, CA: Corwin Press.

Blackburn, B. R. (2008). *Literacy from A to Z: Engaging students in reading, writing, speaking, & listening*. New York: Routledge.

Blackburn, B. R. (2012). *Rigor made easy*. New York: Routledge.

Blackburn, B. R. (2014). *Rigor in your classroom: A toolkit for teachers*. New York: Routledge.

Blackburn, B. R. (2016a). *Classroom instruction from A to Z: How to promote student learning* (2nd edition). New York: Routledge.

Blackburn, B. R. (2016b). *Motivating struggling learners: Ten strategies for student success*. New York: Routledge.

Blackburn, B. R. (2017). *Rigor and assessment in the classroom*. New York: Routledge.

Blackburn, B. R. (2018). *Rigor Is NOT a four-letter word* (3rd edition). New York: Routledge.

Blackburn, B. R., & Witzel, B. (2013). *Rigor for students with special needs*. New York: Routledge.

Blackburn, B. R., & Witzel, B. (2018). *Rigor in the RTI/MTSS classroom*. New York: Routledge.

Blackburn, R., Blackburn, B. R., & Williamson, R. (2017). *Advocacy from A to Z*. New York: Routledge

Brulles, D., Brown, K. L., & Winebrenner, S. (2016). *Differentiated lessons for every learner: Standards-based activities and extensions for middle school*. Waco, TX: Prufrock Press Inc.

Carbaugh, E. M., Doubet, K., & Tomlinson, C. A. (2016). *The differentiated flipped classroom: A practical guide to digital learning*. Thousand Oaks, CA: Corwin Press.

Dodge, J. (2005). *Differentiation in action*. New York: Scholastic.

Doubet, J. A., & Hockett, A. (2015). *Differentiation in middle and high school: Strategies to engage all learners.* Alexandria, VA: Association for Supervision and Curriculum Development.

Doubet, K. J., & Hockett, J. A. (2017). *Differentiation in the elementary grades.* Alexandria, VA: Association of Supervision and Curriculum Development.

DuFour, R., DuFour, R., Easker, R., Many, T. W., & Mattos, M. (2016). *Learning by doing: A handbook for professional learning communities at work* (3rd edition). Bloomington, IN: Solution Tree.

Fogarty, R. J., & Pete, B. M. (2007). *How to differentiate learning: Curriculum, instruction, assessment.* Thousand Oaks, CA: Corwin Press.

Fogarty, R. J., & Pete, B. M. (2011). *Supporting differentiated instruction: A professional learning communities approach.* Bloomington, IL: Solution Tree Press.

Forsten, C., Grant, J., & Hollas, B. (2003). *Differentiating textbooks: Strategies to improve student comprehension & motivation.* Peterborough, NH: Crystal Springs Books.

Garmston, R., & Wellman, B. (2013). *The adaptive school: A sourcebook for developing collaborative groups* (2nd edition). Norwood, MA: Christopher-Gordon.

Gartin, B. C., Murdick, N., Perner, D. E., & Imbeau, M. B. (2016). *Differentiation instruction for the inclusive classroom: Strategies for success.* Arlington, VA: Council for Exceptional Children.

Gregory, G. H. (2008). *Differentiated instructional strategies in practice: Training, implementation, and supervision.* Thousand Oaks, CA: Corwin Press.

Gregory, G. H., & Chapman, C. (2013). *Differentiated instructional strategies: One size doesn't fit all* (3rd edition). Thousand Oaks, CA: Corwin Press.

Gregory, G. H., & Kuzmich, L. (2015). *Student teams that get results: Teaching tools for the differentiated classroom.* New York: Skyhorse Publishing.

Heacox, D. (2002). *Differentiating instruction in the regular classroom: How to reach and teach all learners, grades 3–12.* Minneapolis, MN: Free Spirit Publishing.

Heacox, D. (2017). *Making differentiation a habit: How to ensure success in academically diverse classrooms.* Minneapolis, MN: Free Spirit Publishing.

"Information on Specific Cultural Groups." *BYU McKay School of Education.* Retrieved from education.byu.edu/diversity/culture

Jensen, E. (2013). *Engaging students with poverty in mind: Practical strategies for raising achievement.* Alexandria, VA: Association of Supervision and Curriculum Development.

Langa, M. A., & Yost, J. L. (2007). *Curriculum mapping for differentiated instruction, K–8*. Thousand Oaks, CA: Corwin Press.

Lapp, D. (2016). *Turning the page on complex texts: Differentiated scaffolds for close reading instruction*. Bloomington, IN: Solution Tree Press.

Marzano, R. J., & Pickering, D. J. (2005). *Building academic vocabulary: Teacher's manual*. Alexandria, VA: Association for Supervision and Curriculum Development.

Marzano, R. J., Pickering, D. J., & Pollock, J. E. (2001). *Classroom instruction that works*. Alexandria, VA: Association for Supervision and Curriculum Development.

Maslow, A. (1943). A theory of human motivation. *Psychological Review*.

Miller, D. (2007). *Making the most of small groups: Differentiation for all*. Portland, ME: Stenhouse Publishers.

Reis, S. M., Renzulli, J. S., & Burns, D. E. (2016). *Curriculum compacting: A guide to differentiating curriculum and instruction through enrichment and acceleration* (2nd edition). Waco, TX: Prufrock Press.

Ross, L. (n.d.). Connect with kids and parents of different cultures: How to develop positive relationships with today's diverse families. Retrieved from http://www.scholastic.com/teachers/article/connect-kids-and-parents-different-cultures-0

Small, M. (2010). *Good questions: Great ways to differentiate mathematics instruction*. New York: Teachers College Press.

Smith, G. E., & Throne, S. (2010). *Differentiating instruction with technology in K–5 classrooms*. Eugene, OR: International Society for Technology Integration.

Sousa, D. A., & Tomlinson, C. A. (2011). *Differentiation and the brain: How neuroscience supports the learner-friendly classroom*. Bloomington, IN: Solution Tree Press.

Tomlinson, C. A. (2001). *How to differentiate instruction in mixed-ability classrooms* (2nd edition). Alexandria, VA: Association for Supervision and Curriculum Development.

Tomlinson, C. A. (2006). *Differentiation for gifted and talented students*. Thousand Oaks, CA: Corwin Press.

Tomlinson, C. A. (2015). *Leading for differentiation: Growing teachers who grow kids*. Alexandria, VA: Association for Supervision and Curriculum Development.

Tomlinson, C. A. (2017). *How to differentiate instruction in academically diverse classrooms*. Alexandria, VA: Association for Supervision and Curriculum Development.

Tomlinson, C. A., & Imbeau, M. B. (2011). *Leading and managing a differentiated classroom*. Alexandria, VA: Association for Supervision and Curriculum Development.

Tomlinson, C. A., & McTighe, J. (2006). *Integrating differentiated instruction & understanding by design: Connecting content and kids.* Alexandria, VA: Association for Supervision and Curriculum Development.

Tomlinson, C. A., & Moon, T. R. (2013). *Assessment and student success in a differentiated classroom.* Alexandria, VA: Association for Supervision and Curriculum Development.

Tomlinson, C. A., & Strickland, C. A. (2005). *Differentiation in practice a resource guide for differentiating curriculum: Grades 9–12.* Alexandria, VA: Association for Supervision and Curriculum Development.

Tomlinson, C. A., et al. (2008). *The parallel curriculum: A design to develop learner potential and challenge advanced learners.* Thousand Oaks, CA: Corwin Press.

Williamson, R., & Blackburn, B. (2017). *Rigor in your school: A toolkit for leaders* (2nd edition). New York: Routledge.

Wormeli, R. (2006). *Fair isn't always equal: Assessing & grading in the differentiated classroom.* Portland, ME: Stenhouse Publishers.

Wormeli, R. (n.d.). Busting myths about differentiation. Portland, ME: Great Schools Partnership. Retrieved from https://www. greatschoolspartnership.org/wp-content/uploads/2017/01/ Busting-Myths-About-Differentiated-Instruction-1.pdf

Wormeli, R., & Tomlinson, C. A. (2007). *Differentiation: From planning to practice, grades 6–12.* Portland, ME: Stenhouse Publishers.